Joyce Appleby on *Thomas Jefferson*

Louis Auchincloss on *Theodore Roosevelt*

Jean Baker on *James Buchanan*

H. W. Brands on *Woodrow Wilson*

Douglas Brinkley on *Gerald Ford*

James MacGregor Burns and Susan Dunn on *George Washington*

Robert Dallek on *James Monroe*

John W. Dean on *Warren Harding*

John Patrick Diggins on *John Adams*

E. L. Doctorow on *Abraham Lincoln*

Henry F. Graff on *Grover Cleveland*

Roy Jenkins on *Franklin Delano Roosevelt*

Zachary Karabell on *Chester A. Arthur*

William E. Leuchtenburg on *Herbert Hoover*

Robert V. Remini on *John Quincy Adams*

John Seigenthaler on *James K. Polk*

Hans L. Trefousse on *Rutherford B. Hayes*

Tom Wicker on *Dwight D. Eisenhower*

Ted Widmer on *Martin Van Buren*

Sean Wilentz on *Andrew Jackson*

Garry Wills on *James Madison*

*Ben Butler: The South Called Him Beast*
*Benjamin Franklin Wade: Radical Republican from Ohio*
*The Radical Republicans: Lincoln's Vanguard for Racial Justice*
*Impeachment for a President*
*Andrew Johnson: A Biography*
*Carl Schurz: A Biography*
*Thaddeus Stevens: Nineteenth-Century Egalitarian*
*Germany and American Neutrality, 1939–1940*
*Pearl Harbor: The Continuing Controversy*

# Rutherford B. Hayes

Hans L. Trefousse

# Rutherford B. Hayes

**THE AMERICAN PRESIDENTS**

ARTHUR M. SCHLESINGER, JR., GENERAL EDITOR

Times Books

HENRY HOLT AND COMPANY, NEW YORK

Times Books
Henry Holt and Company, LLC
*Publishers since 1866*
115 West 18th Street
New York, New York 10011

Henry Holt® is a registered trademark of Henry Holt and Company, LLC.

LIBRARY OF CONGRESS CATALOGING-IN-PUBLICATION DATA

Trefousse, Hans Louis.
  Rutherford B. Hayes / Hans L. Trefousse ; Arthur M. Schlesinger, Jr.,
general editor.—1st ed.
    p. cm. — (The American presidents series)
  Includes bibliographical references (p. ) and index
  ISBN: 0-8050-6907-0
  1. Hayes, Rutherford Birchard, 1822–1893. 2. Presidents—United States—
Biography. 3. Reconstruction. 4. United States—Politics and government—
1877–1881. I. Title. II. American presidents series (Times Books (Firm))
E682 .T74 2002
973.8'3'092—dc21
[B]                                                              2002069577

Henry Holt books are available for special promotions and premiums.
For details contact: Director, Special Markets.

First Edition 2002

Printed in the United States of America
1   3   5   7   9   10   8   6   4   2

# Contents

# Editor's Note

The president is the central player in the American political order. That would seem to contradict the intentions of the Founding Fathers. Remembering the horrid example of the British monarchy, they invented a separation of powers in order, as Justice Brandeis later put it, "to preclude the exercise of arbitrary power." Accordingly, they divided the government into three allegedly equal and coordinate branches—the executive, the legislative, and the judiciary.

But a system based on the tripartite separation of powers has an inherent tendency toward inertia and stalemate. One of the three branches must take the initiative if the system is to move. The executive branch alone is structurally capable of taking that initiative. The Founders must have sensed this when they accepted Alexander Hamilton's proposition in the Seventieth Federalist that "energy in the executive is a leading character in the definition of good government." They thus envisaged a strong president—but within an equally strong system of constitutional accountability. (The term *imperial presidency* arose in the 1970s to describe the situation when the balance between power and accountability is upset in favor of the executive.)

The American system of self-government thus comes to focus in the presidency—"the vital place of action in the system," as Woodrow Wilson put it. Henry Adams, himself the great-grandson and grandson of presidents as well as the most brilliant of American historians, said that the American president "resembles the commander of a ship at sea. He must have a helm to grasp, a course to steer, a port to seek." The men in the White House (thus far only men, alas) in steering their chosen courses have shaped our destiny as a nation.

Biography offers an easy education in American history, rendering the past more human, more vivid, more intimate, more accessible, more connected to ourselves. Biography reminds us that presidents are not supermen. They are human beings too, worrying about decisions, attending to wives and children, juggling balls in the air and putting on their pants one leg at a time. Indeed, as Emerson contended, "There is properly no history; only biography."

Presidents serve us as inspirations, and they also serve us as warnings. They provide bad examples as well as good. The nation, the Supreme Court has said, has "no right to expect that it will always have wise and humane rulers, sincerely attached to the principles of the Constitution. Wicked men, ambitious of power, with hatred of liberty and contempt of law, may fill the place once occupied by Washington and Lincoln."

The men in the White House express the ideal and the values, the frailties and the flaws, of the voters who send them there. It is altogether natural that we should want to know more about the virtues and the vices of the fellows we have elected to govern us. As we know more about them, we will know more about ourselves. The French political philosopher Joseph de Maistre said, "Every nation has the government it deserves."

At the start of the twenty-first century, forty-two men have made it to the oval office. (George W. Bush is counted our forty-third president, because Grover Cleveland, who served nonconsecutive terms, is counted twice.) Of the parade of presidents, a dozen or so lead the polls periodically conducted by historians and political scientists. What makes a great president?

Great presidents possess, or are possessed by, a vision of an ideal America. Their passion, as they grasp the helm, is to set the ship of state on the right course toward the port they seek. Great presidents also have a deep psychic connection with the needs, anxieties, dreams of people. "I do not believe," said Wilson, "that any man can lead who does not act . . . under the impulse of a profound sympathy with those whom he leads—a sympathy which is insight—an insight which is of the heart rather than of the intellect."

"All of our great presidents," said Franklin D. Roosevelt, "were leaders of thought at a time when certain ideas in the life of the nation had to be clarified." So Washington incarnated the idea of federal union, Jefferson and Jackson the idea of democracy, Lincoln union and freedom, Cleveland rugged honesty. Theodore Roosevelt and Wilson, said FDR, were both "moral leaders, each in his own way and his own time, who used the presidency as a pulpit."

To succeed, presidents must not only have a port to seek but they must convince Congress and the electorate that it is a port worth seeking. Politics in a democracy is ultimately an educational process, an adventure in persuasion and consent. Every president stands in Theodore Roosevelt's bully pulpit.

The greatest presidents in the scholars' rankings, Washington, Lincoln, and Franklin Roosevelt, were leaders who confronted and overcame the republic's greatest crises. Crisis widens presidential opportunities for bold and imaginative action. But it does not guarantee presidential greatness. The crisis of secession did not spur Buchanan or the crisis of depression spur Hoover to creative leadership. Their inadequacies in the face of crisis allowed Lincoln and the second Roosevelt to show the difference individuals make to history. Still, even in the absence of first-order crisis, forceful and persuasive presidents—Jackson, Theodore Roosevelt, Ronald Reagan—are able to impose their own priorities on the country.

The diverse drama of the presidency offers a fascinating set of tales. Biographies of American presidents constitute a chronicle of wisdom and folly, nobility and pettiness, courage and cunning, forthrightness and deceit, quarrel and consensus. The turmoil perennially swirling around the White House illuminates the heart of the American democracy.

It is the aim of the American Presidents series to present the grand panorama of our chief executives in volumes compact enough for the busy reader, lucid enough for the student, authoritative enough for the scholar. Each volume offers a distillation of character and career. I hope that these lives will give readers some understanding of the pitfalls and potentialities of the presidency and also of the responsibilities of citizenship. Truman's famous sign—"The buck stops here"—tells only half the story. Citizens cannot escape the ultimate responsibility. It is in the voting booth, not on the presidential desk, that the buck finally stops.

—Arthur M. Schlesinger, Jr.

# Rutherford B. Hayes

# Introduction

"The iniquity in Florida" wrote the *New York Sun* about the presidential election, not in the year 2000, but in 1876. The newspaper was referring to that year's disputed balloting, which had pitted the Republican governor of Ohio, Rutherford B. Hayes, and his New York running mate, William A. Wheeler, against the Democratic governor of New York, Samuel J. Tilden, and his running mate, Thomas A. Hendricks of Indiana. As in 2000, the controversy was in part because of a dispute about African-American votes, not only in Florida but in other Southern states as well. The matter was finally settled, as in 2000, but in the nineteenth century, unlike in the twentieth and twenty-first, the dispute was not permitted to rest. During his entire term of office, his opponents, referring to Hayes as the "Fraudulent President," continued to question his legitimacy and attempted to replace him.

Who was this source of contention, destined to become the nineteenth president of the United States? As one of the Gilded Age's chief executives, he is generally considered less important than the emerging industrialists and businessmen of the era. Yet, as his biographers, especially Ari Hoogenboom and Harry Barnard have shown, this verdict is unfair. Hoogenboom called him a precursor of the Progressive movement, "remarkable both for his independence and his savvy." Barnard thought he personified "the educated but typical, middle-of-the-road American of his day," and both gave him high marks for his restoration of the powers of the presidency. And they were right. Hayes was not one of the greatest presidents, but he managed to serve out his originally disputed term without scandal and with considerable competence. He deserves to be remembered.

# Background and Youth

Hayes had little in common with George W. Bush, his twenty-first-century successor. Not only was his father not a public figure, let alone a president, but his father, Rutherford Hayes, Jr., died before the birth of his son. A New Englander born in West Brattleboro, Vermont, he descended from a long line of Presbyterians who had come from Scotland in 1625 to settle in Connecticut. He had a common school education, had clerked in a store in Wilmington, Vermont, and then went into partnership with his brother-in-law Joseph Noyes in a store in Dummerston. Leaving for Ohio in 1817 with eight thousand dollars, he settled in the town of Delaware in that state to farm, trade, and invest in a distillery, Lamb & Hayes, a strange investment for the father of a future president who kept liquor out of the White House. An active Presbyterian, he was a strong supporter of education, both religious and secular. He died in July 1822 of a fever.

Hayes's mother, Sophia Birchard, was also a descendant of an old New England family, whose paternal ancestor had arrived in America from England in 1634. Her father, Roger Birchard, was born in Connecticut and was a retail merchant in Wilmington, Vermont, who died at forty-five years of age. At her husband's death in the summer of 1822, she inherited some land near Delaware, as well as an unfinished brick house in town. Rutherford Birchard, named after both parents, had been born on October 4, 1822, and moved into the new house the following year. It was a two-story brick dwelling on the northeast corner of William and Winter Streets, with the kitchen in an adjoining old one-story frame building fronting on Winter Street, and was not finished until 1828. At first, short on resources, the family had little furniture for its new home: a new bureau and stand, plain wood-bottomed chairs, a gilt-frame looking glass, a good carpet, and cheap curtains for the parlor. The family consisted of the mother; the boy; Fanny, an older sister; and a brother, who drowned in 1825 while skating. Hayes's mother's cousin, Arcena Smith, lived with the family, as did her brother, Sardis Birchard, a lifelong bachelor. This uncle, a businessman and banker, became his guardian and virtual father figure. It was he who took charge of his nephew's education, provided funds, and in frequent letters gave him valuable advice after he moved to Lower Sandusky in 1827.

Mrs. Hayes's income was derived from the rent of a farm some ten miles north of town, and Rud, as he was called, and his sister Fanny, whom he adored, and with whom he played and later steadily corresponded, loved to visit it. The tenants gave them colored eggs filled with sugar at Easter, pet birds, rabbits, and turtles' eggs, while the children busied themselves with sugar-making, cider-making, and the gathering of hickory and walnuts.

Rud was a sickly child whose survival was at first doubtful. It was Fanny who was his protector and nurse, leading him about the garden and on short visits to neighbors. He was able to reciprocate when she in turn fell ill, giving her little rides upon a sled during her recovery. Together they boarded with Arcena and her new husband, Thomas Wasson, when their mother went to nurse their sick uncle, and it was Wasson who sent them to the local district school in Delaware, run by a fierce Yankee schoolmaster who was notorious for his floggings. In spite of their pleadings to be taken out, Wasson refused. When his mother returned, Rud, in 1834, took his first trip, a journey to his relatives in Vermont and Massachusetts, which he thoroughly enjoyed. The next year he visited his uncle in Lower Sandusky, thus starting a lifelong habit of enthusiastic traveling.

In 1836 Rud was sent to a new school, the Norwalk Seminary in Ohio. The seminary, a Methodist school run by the Reverend Jonathan E. Chaplin, was more to Hayes's liking than the previous institution, although he missed his sister very much. He was not fazed by his studies; on composition day, he wrote an essay about Liberty, and on speaking day, delivered a eulogy on Lord Chatham, both well done. In the next year, he was transferred to Isaac Webb's school in Middletown, Connecticut, where, with his friend William Lane, he studied Latin and Greek. Although at first it was hard to keep up with the class, he quickly succeeded. He was very pleased with this school, as well as its director. Getting up at 6:30, he breakfasted, said prayers, and started his classes at nine. Dinner was at twelve. On Saturday afternoons he took long hikes, and he also began a study of French. That he was successful was clearly recognized by Webb, who wrote to Sardis Birchard, "Rutherford has applied himself industriously to his studies and has maintained a constant and correct deportment. I think he will avail himself of the advantage of an education and fully meet the just anticipations of his friends. He is well informed, has good sense, and is respected and esteemed by his companions. He is strictly economical and regular in his habits and has established a very favorable character among us."

Despite Webb's belief that he was too young for college, Hayes was anxious to go, and in 1838 entered Kenyon College at Gambier, Ohio. There, too, he established an excellent record. Enjoying his college career, he made several lasting friendships, among them future Supreme Court Justice Stanley Matthews, future Michigan Congressman Rowland E. Trowbridge, future Ohio Attorney General Christopher Wolcott, and future Texas politician Guy M. Bryan. The Texan, later a lawyer and state legislator, became a particularly close companion with whom he remained on the most friendly terms almost to the day of his death, in spite of their differences during and prior to the Civil War. It was also at Kenyon that he started his diary, an invaluable source for his career, which he continued to keep to the end of his life. Joining the Philomathesian Society, a literary and theatrical organization, he was able to engage in his favorite pastimes of reading and partaking in discussions. With a number of friends he founded a friendship club, Phi Zeta, which adopted as its motto, *Phila Zoe,* "Friendship for Life." At the same time, he perfected his speaking ability, delivering speeches to the society and to the college. For vacations, he generally went to Columbus, where his sister, now married to William A. Platt, a jeweler and businessman, had established her home. One of several speakers on graduation day in 1842, he chose as his topic "College Life" and discussed its many advantages. As valedictorian, he addressed the school president, whom he praised for his closeness to the students, the faculty, and his fellow students.

In view of the fact that he intended to become an attorney after leaving Kenyon, he began reading law at the office of Sparrow & Matthews in Columbus. Studying Blackston and Chillingworth while also learning German, he absorbed a great deal of legal lore. His uncle, however, thought he ought to have a regular legal education and insisted that he go to Harvard. Thus, in 1843, traveling by way of Buffalo and Niagara Falls—which, after an initial disappointment, he admired—he entered the Cambridge law school.

He liked Harvard as much as he had enjoyed Kenyon. "The advantages of the law school are as great as I expected to find them, and the means of passing time pleasantly even greater," he wrote to his uncle. Because of his previous studies, he was able to attend all the recitations without overexertion, and he was particularly influenced by lectures of Supreme Court Justice Joseph Story and the famous lawyer, Professor Simon Greenleaf. These two excellent teachers' style and learning became a model for the young student.

He followed a strict daily routine. Rising at six, he exercised before breakfast, then, on Mondays, studied law until eleven, German till two, moot court till seven, and in the evening wrote out his notes while turning to Whatley and Chillingworth. On Tuesdays, he perused the law till one, devoted the afternoon to Hoffman's *Law Studies*, and took up the law again in the evening. Wednesdays were much like Mondays until two, then he busied himself with Hoffman and moot court questions, and spent the evening in the same way as on Tuesdays. On Thursdays, he again studied law till one, German in the afternoon, and passed the evening as on Tuesdays. On Fridays, it was once more law and German till two, and the afternoon and evening were given over to bringing up arrears. On Saturdays, he again gave his attention for two hours to the law, and then finally enjoyed some sports. On Sundays, he went to church and saw friends.

But his stay in Cambridge did not consist entirely of study. He had an opportunity to hear many famous orators, among them John Quincy Adams, George Bancroft, Henry Wadsworth Longfellow, and Daniel Webster. While Adams seemed to be too extreme on the slavery question, he thought him "truly a most formidable man." Bancroft appeared to be one of the most interesting speakers he had ever heard; Longfellow, who spoke on modern languages, pleased him with his style and manner; and Webster apparently deserved the epithet, the "godlike." He was introduced to the theater and saw *Hamlet*. Though he dreaded the loss of time, he also found vacations in Vermont and Columbus pleasant diversions.

Hayes left Harvard at the end of his third semester in February 1845. After admission to the bar in Marietta, Ohio, he decided to settle in Lower Sandusky, soon to be called Fremont, where he had contacts. His uncle Sardis and his cousin John R. Pease were living there, and Professor Greenleaf had advised young lawyers not to settle in large cities. Rooming with his cousin Pease and forming a partnership with Ralph P. Buckland, who after some difficulties became a friend, he entered upon his profession. As Ward D. Marchman, the author of an excellent essay on Hayes's legal career, has chronicled, he was soon retained by the state in a suit to recover certain debts from a sheriff. When Pease's wallet and other property, as well as his own watch, were stolen, he successfully prosecuted the perpetrator. Falling sick in 1847, Hayes considered joining the army in Mexico to benefit from the climate there, but his doctors advised against it, and he took a trip to New England instead. Then, in company with his uncle, he went to Texas to visit his friend Guy Bryan. Lengthy horseback rides and adventurous hunts, as well as the renewed companionship with Bryan, made this vacation gratifying. On his return, having heard from his friend George Hoadly that Cincinnati was a growing city of 120,000 people and offered many opportunities, he decided to move to the city, where he established his permanent home in 1849.

Opening his office in January 1850, at Third Street between Maine and Syracuse, like most young lawyers he at first had to wait in vain for business, but in February he received his first retainer of $5 from a coal trader to defend a suit in the commercial court. By March, he had ten new claims in commercial court, and later that month had established himself well enough to be able to travel to Fremont and Columbus, returning by rail by way of Tiffin and Springfield, then by stage to Dayton and by packet to St. Mary's and Cincinnati.

Cincinnati provided many opportunities that had been missing in Fremont. Hayes joined a literary club that provided him with opportunities to listen to speeches and to speak himself. He heard famous orators, who often came to town, and was most impressed with Ralph Waldo Emerson, who, among other topics, spoke on natural aristocracy and the institutions of England. At first he thought Emerson showed himself a close observer rather than a profound thinker, but he listened to him again and again, invited him to the literary club, bought all his works, and gradually became convinced of "the infinite worth of his writings." Theodore Parker, "the notorious Christian infidel," as he called him, spoke on Progress, The True and False Ideas of a Gentleman, and Woman. Hayes found him witty and a man of sounder judgment than he had supposed. Henry Ward Beecher, the illustrious Brooklyn abolitionist minister, who discoursed on The Beautiful in Nature and Art, seemed pithy and eloquent, and Hayes liked him better than he had ever thought before. Edward Everett, who held forth on George Washington, appeared to Hayes "the best specimen of a refined, scholarly, eloquent holiday orator." The young lawyer was fascinated by all of these speakers.

His practice continued to pick up, and, as luck would have it, he became involved in two murder cases that provided him with extensive publicity. The first of these, "the criminal case of the term," as Hayes wrote, concerned Nancy Farrer, a deformed girl who had poisoned a number of her employers. He took part in the trial after serving as counsel for the defense in a larceny case concerning one Samuel Cunningham. The defendant was convicted, but the prosecuting attorney as well as Judge R. B. Warden paid the young defense counsel handsome compliments. He so impressed the judge that Warden appointed him to the Farrer case, which he thought would give him a better opportunity to exhibit "whatever pith" was in him than any other case in which he had been involved, and it did. Thoroughly researching the girl's background, he found details that were helpful to the defense. Her father had been a drunkard who committed suicide, while the mother believed herself to be the bride of Jesus Christ and a Mormon prophetess. An insanity defense was obviously called for, and though the case was originally lost, counsel's argument was again impressive. As quoted by Charles Richard Williams in his extensive biography, Hayes, stressing the defendant's mental state, said: "The calamity of insanity is one which may touch very nearly the happiness of the best of our citizens. We all know that in one of its

thousand forms it has carried grief and agony unspeakable into
many a happy home, and we must all wish to see such rules in
regard to it established as would satisfy an intelligent man if, instead
of this friendless girl, his own sister or daughter were on trial. And
surely to establish such rules will be a most noble achievement of
that intelligence and reason which God has given to you, but he has
denied to her whose fate is in your hands." After the girl was convicted and sentenced to death, he obtained a writ of error and carried the case to the state supreme court. A probate court of inquiry
finally sent her to an insane asylum, and his success in saving the
prisoner from the gallows did not go unnoticed, particularly because
she was a woman.

The second case also involved a poisoner, James Summons, who
had killed several relatives while trying to do away with his parents.
Hayes continued to represent the defendant after his previous
attorney became inebriated, and after several trials complicated by
the death of the prosecution's chief witness, succeeded in obtaining
a divided opinion in the state supreme court. Eventually Governor
Salmon P. Chase commuted the death sentence to life imprisonment. Thus the rising attorney contributed to saving this murderer
from execution as well. In another case concerning the assassination of a lover by a jealous husband, he was less successful, and,
much to his disgust, had to witness the culprit's execution. He also
represented his uncle in several trials, one an ejectment effort by
Thomas E. Boswell against Sardis Birchard and his partner Rodol-
phus Dickinson concerning a parcel of land by the lower rapids of
the Sandusky River. Though the plaintiff's lawyer, Brice J. Bartlett,
won the case, it was eventually settled when Bartlett decided to sell
the property. The other matter involved Sardis's effort to obtain an
injunction to stop the Junction Railroad Company from building
a bridge across Sandusky Bay. Though the injunction was finally
granted, in the long run it proved impossible to stop the development of rail connections across the bay.

In December 1853, Richard M. Corwine offered Hayes second

place in his firm among four partners. He hesitated, but when the two other partners finally left, he accepted a partnership, which included his friend William K. Rogers, and on December 26 the new firm of Corwine, Hayes & Rogers was launched. It was a successful enterprise.

In the meantime Hayes had fallen in love. Overcoming his shyness with girls, in 1847 he had become interested in a Connecticut girl from Norwich named Fanny Perkins, whom he courted both in Ohio and in New England. She came from an old New England family, but her mother did not want her to move to Ohio, and the affair ended. Then his attention turned to two other girls, Frances Kelley of Columbus and Lucy Ware Webb of Chillicothe, who had moved to Cincinnati. The daughter of Dr. James and Maria Cook Webb, Lucy, like Rud, had lost her father at an early age, when he had gone to Kentucky to free some slaves, only to fall sick and die. The attractive, hazel-eyed young woman with dark, glossy hair went to Ohio Wesleyan University in Delaware, where Hayes first met her. Well educated, charming, and possessed of the Puritan determination of her maternal ancestry, Lucy was extremely popular. As Harry Barnard has shown, Hayes soon decided that in spite of her attractions Frances Kelley was not for him. Lucy, on the other hand, attracted him more and more.

He finally made up his mind. In June 1851, sitting in a rush-bottom rocking chair in front of Lucy, ensconced on a short sofa, he grasped her hand and said, "I love you." After some hesitation and after he had repeated his declaration, she replied, "I must confess, I like you very well," and their faith was plighted for life. One week later, when he was in Columbus, he reaffirmed his passion for her. As he wrote to her, "To think that *that* lovely vision is an actual, living, breathing being, and is loved by me, and loves me in return, and will one day be my bride—my abiding, forgiving, trustful, loving wife—to make my happy home blessed indeed with her cheerful smile and silver voice and warm true heart! I don't know, Lucy dearest, what you think of it, but—if I *could* quote Tom Moore I would, 'If there be an

Elysium of bliss *it is this it is this.*'" When she left in August, he not only told her that he was very lonely without her but reminded her of their first meeting in Delaware in 1847. He wrote to her every few days and mentioned that he had talked to her mother. When she returned in October, he thought she was looking more beautiful than ever. Whenever they were separated, the two lovers wrote lengthy letters to each other. When he went to Columbus the next summer, he let her know that people were talking about them and their impending marriage, and in the beginning of December, he was finally ready to tell his uncle that the wedding plans were set. The ceremony, performed by Dr. L. D. McCabe, of Ohio Wesleyan University, took place on December 30, 1852, at Lucy's house, in the presence of his sister Fanny and her daughter Laura, Uncle Sardis, two members of Phi Zeta, as well as Lucy's family and some thirty invited guests.

The marriage, lasting some forty years, could not have been happier. A highly intelligent and accomplished woman, Lucy in many ways became the mainstay of his life. Her outgoing ways, her fetching smile, and her social graces were of great advantage to her husband. "Few men in this most important relation of life have been as blessed as I have been," he wrote after she had died. "From early mature manhood to the threshold of old age I have enjoyed her society in the most intimate of all relations." The newlyweds moved in with Lucy's mother, an association he found most agreeable. In February 1853, he mused that he had been married for almost two months and that the "dear friend" who was to share the joys and ills of life with him was growing steadily dearer and nearer to him. "A better wife I never hope to have," he concluded.

Rud and Lucy were blessed with eight children, seven boys and one girl, of whom four boys and the girl survived. The first one, Birchard, Birch for short, arrived in 1853, to his father's great pleasure. The second, Webb, a healthy little black-haired boy destined to become his father's secretary, was born in 1856; the third, Rutherford

Platt, generally called Ruddy, in 1858; the only daughter, Fanny, the apple of her father's eye, came into the world in 1869; and the last surviving son, Scott Russell, two years later. Joseph, born in 1861, George Crook, in 1864, and Manning Force, in 1873, died as infants.

During all this time, Hayes had always been interested in politics. A convinced Whig even while still at Kenyon College, he avidly followed the 1840 campaign pitting General William Henry Harrison and his running mate, John Tyler, against President Martin Van Buren. "Tippecanoe and Tyler too," was the Whig watchword, and Hayes, rooting for the Whig candidates, was cheered by Harrison's success in state after state. Then, on November 5, he was able to write happily, "The long agony is over. The 'whirlwind' has swept over the land and General Harrison is undoubtedly elected President. I never was more elated by anything in my life."

The elation did not last long. Harrison died a few weeks after his inauguration, and Vice President John Tyler of Virginia became his successor. Pro-slavery and a determined believer in states' rights, as well as a strict interpretation of the Constitution, Tyler vetoed Henry Clay's measures to reestablish some type of a national bank, an act that led to his expulsion from the Whig party. While Hayes claimed that he was much less addicted to politics and criticized both Whigs and Democrats for their attitudes toward the president, he still favored the Whigs and thought that they ought to stay united. Continuing to profess a lack of concern, he seemingly stood aloof from the elections of 1842, but two years later he became a determined supporter of Henry Clay and was sadly disappointed when his hero was defeated. Yet he believed that the Democrats—the Locos, as he and other Whigs called them—would soon split apart about the question of the annexation of Texas, the tariff, and such rival personalities as John C. Calhoun and Thomas Hart Benton. Rejoicing in the Whigs' victory in Ohio in 1846, two years later he was an enthusiastic backer of the Whig candidate Zachary

Taylor, for whom he campaigned and whose victory greatly encouraged him, and by 1849 he had become a member of the Lower Sandusky Whig Central Committee.

By that time, the slavery issue had become ever more important. While always mildly opposed to the institution, Hayes at first did not sympathize with abolitionists, whom he had heard Joseph Story denounce at Harvard. But during the Texas trip, he mused that, pleasant as life was on the local plantations, he doubted whether "a person of Northern education could so far forget his home-bred notions and feelings as to be thoroughly Southern on the subject of slavery." In fact, his mother had long been a determined opponent of the institution. Freeing her father's slaves, she said she would take in washing to support the family before she would sell a slave. As far as he was concerned, much as he sympathized with Henry Clay, he had no use for the Kentuckian's Compromise of 1850. Its pro-slavery provisions of a strong fugitive slave law, the maintenance of slavery in the District of Columbia, the opening up of territories to possible tolerance of the institution through popular sovereignty, the right of the settlers to decide on the question, and the assumption of the Texan debt seemed to favor the South, although the North benefited by the admission of California as a free state, the abolition of the slave trade in the federal district, and the reduction of Texas's borders. All in all, the compromise was anathema to many Northerners. Hayes doubted its value even while it was still being debated. When Daniel Webster in his Seventh of March speech supported the measure, the Ohioan regretted that one of his genius had taken a course so contrary to his past course. Expressing little confidence in Webster's integrity, in his diary Hayes quoted James Greenleaf Whittier's poem, "Ichabod," the poet's attack on the statesman. To his friend Bryan he wrote that Texas asked for too much territory in New Mexico, a land grab resented in the North as an effort to extend slave territory.

He was soon to become more active in antislavery politics. After he had settled in Cincinnati, he took on a number of fugitive slave cases, the most notable of which was that of Rosetta Armstrong, as Watt P. Marchman has shown. Armstrong, a slave taken through Ohio on behalf of her master, the Reverend Henry M. Dennison, was detained in Columbus. Her master sued to recapture her; she was freed and rearrested; and Hayes, together with Salmon P. Chase, then procured her freedom.

However, still an active Whig, in 1852 he became an enthusiastic supporter of General Winfield Scott. The general, in full uniform, had come to Cincinnati in April 1851 on the Pittsburgh packet. Seeing him for the first time, Hayes, impressed by the noble-looking soldier, thought he would make a good president. And when Scott was nominated in 1852 to run against Franklin Pierce, Rud naturally spoke for him. Although hoping for the best, he was not too sanguine about the outcome of the election. Nevertheless, he thought a victory for Pierce would make the annexation of Cuba with its slave system the question of the day and possibly improve the chances of the opposition in Ohio. The Whigs' subsequent defeat he considered a veritable Waterloo, which it proved to be. He himself would soon join the party's Republican successor.

The new organization was the result of the repeal of the time-honored Missouri Compromise of 1820, which had outlawed slavery north of 36° 30'. By allowing the inhabitants of the territories of Kansas and Nebraska to decide whether or not to permit slavery and thus making possible the spread of the institution, the measure infuriated a great number of Northerners. Consequently, various political groupings appeared, some called Republican, some named Fusion or People's party, and Hayes was active in organizing the Cincinnati branch. Though not prejudiced himself, he even sought to collaborate with the anti-Catholic Know-Nothings to further the chances of his partner Corwine for state attorney general and was a delegate to the new party's state convention. In 1856, a presidential election year, he was offered a judgeship, which, uncertain of electoral success, he declined. Avidly supporting John C. Frémont, the Republican candidate against the Democrat James Buchanan, he was afraid of "the probable defeat of the cause of freedom," and when his fears became fact, he was not surprised. Glad that he himself had not been running, he believed that though beaten, Frémont had done well. "I am enlisted for the war," he wrote, and studied the history of the British struggle against the slave trade.

In spite of his domestic bliss, the year 1856 was one of great sorrow for him. His sister Fanny died in July after giving birth to still-born twins. "My dear sister, my beloved Fanny, is dead," he mourned. "The dearest friend of childhood, the affectionate adviser, the confidante of all my life, the one I loved best, is gone, alas! Never to be seen again on earth." He had traveled to Columbus when she was already mortally ill but returned when she seemed to be gaining slightly. Deeply affected by her demise, he soon transferred his love for his sister to her daughter Laura.

Politically, he remained active. A delegate to the Union convention in 1857, he was nominated for Congress but withdrew. Nevertheless, the *Cincinnati Enquirer* wrote that the Democrats feared him much more than the eventual nominee, who, despite Hayes's prediction to the contrary, finally lost. Though not running for Congress in 1858, he nevertheless obtained his first political office that year, when, after the incumbent died, the city council elected him city solicitor. He was lucky; his election was due to the vote of one Democrat, who, to break a deadlock, finally cast his ballot for him. Well satisfied with his office, which was much more profitable than the judgeship, paying thirty-five hundred dollars instead of fifteen hundred dollars per annum, he was reelected in the popular election in April, and again in 1860. He could take pride in his popularity and his increasing public recognition; by February 1860, he had disposed of 187 cases for the city, many of them successfully. But in spite of his two victories, he was defeated for reelection the following year in a general resurgence of the Democrats as Union savers.

Although active in the new party, he nevertheless realized that, in order to succeed, it would have to be as a moderate. Accordingly, he tried to inform Abraham Lincoln, who was about to visit the city, that the local group was not the Republican but only the "opposition party." Still, he rejoiced in the election of the radical antislavery leader Salmon P. Chase to the United States Senate and the Republican William Dennison to the governorship. As for Lincoln, Hayes was reassured by the information that the Illinois statesman was an old Clay Whig, "of Kentucky parentage, with a wholesome dislike of Locofocoism."

During the vital campaign of 1860, Hayes served as vice chairman of the Republican Executive Committee of Hamilton County. The nomination of four candidates—Lincoln for the Republicans, Douglas for the popular sovereignty Democrats, John C. Breckinridge for the pro-slavery Democrats, as well as John Bell for the Constitutional Unionists—made him think the election would probably go to the House. All in all, he was not optimistic. Writing to his uncle, he informed him that he was unable to arouse much interest in the contest. Though there was contempt for Douglas for what he called his recent "demagoguery," he was not sure that Lincoln could win. Fusion between opponents in New Jersey and Pennsylvania might defeat him. After the October elections resulted in Republican victories in Ohio and Pennsylvania, he was more hopeful, and on Election Day, considering the problem confronting the Union, he felt that South Carolina's threatened secession might either encourage the other slave states to follow suit or cause the influence of the more conservative ones to draw the ultra states back into the Union. At all events, he thought the time had come to test this question. "If the threats are meant," he wrote, "then it is time the Union was dissolved or the traitors crushed out."

During the next few weeks, his diary was strangely silent about the secession crisis. By January, however, he passionately denounced compromise: "Civil war and disunion are at hand," he wrote, "and yet I fear disunion and civil war less than compromise." He thought the nation could recover from these evils, and the free states alone would make a glorious nation stretching from the Atlantic to the Pacific—"free—all free," as he put it. He was not at all apprehensive.

Believing it would not be necessary to subdue most of the slave states, only those necessary for a decent boundary, he thought this would not require a long war and the end result would be two nations. On January 27, when six states had already seceded, he wrote, "Let them go." If the Union were dissolved it would not prove that free government was a failure, merely that the experiment of uniting free and slave states could not work. After all, popular government had been successful in all the free states, and even in a majority of the slaveholding states.

In February, the president-elect came to Cincinnati on his way to Washington, and Hayes was wholly captivated by "this typical American" and his moderate views. Still opposed to the abolitionists, he was satisfied by Lincoln's refusal to cater to the violently antislavery German turners, as the gymnasts called themselves. His final verdict was, "He [Lincoln] undoubtedly is shrewd, able, and possesses strength in reserve." His characterization was much more accurate than that of many others at that time.

Having been defeated for reelection as city solicitor, Hayes formed a new partnership with Leopold Markbreit, the brother of the German-American political leader Friedrich Hassaurek, a connection he hoped would give him access to the large German-American community in the city. However, the partnership would not be a long-lasting one. The war interrupted it.

By this time Hayes was a well-built young man, 5' 8½" tall, with an open countenance and blue eyes, sandy hair, and the beginnings of a beard. A man of firm ideas, he had a good opinion of himself, was ambitious, but tried to hide these facts. He loved to travel, went to Niagara Falls, Canada, New England, New York, and the middle states, as well as to Virginia and Texas. And, having overcome his early shyness with girls when he found Lucy, he was able to enjoy fully his friendship with females. Above all, he was always moderate. His long friendship with Guy Bryan was never endangered by the sectional conflict. He congratulated his friend upon becoming a state legislator and even encouraged him to run for the United

States Senate. Although informing Bryan that he was leaning toward Republicanism, he added, "Still we shall not quarrel about politics, even if we differ as of old." In his last letter before going off to war, he insisted that he knew they would remain friends, much as they might differ about the war. It was this type of feeling that was to become so prominent during his presidency.

# 2

## Civil War

In many ways, the Civil War and Hayes's part in it became the experience of which he was most proud—more so than the presidency. Though at first opposed to warfare, he did so well during the conflict that his principal biographer, Ari Hoogenboom, entitled his life, *Rutherford B. Hayes: Warrior and President*. His characterization was correct; Hayes's military career was most successful.

Hayes's original thoughts about the probability of the permanent division of the Union soon disappeared after the attack on Fort Sumter. "How relieved we were to have a Government again," he wrote in his diary shortly afterward. Made chairman of the committee on resolutions of a union mass meeting in Cincinnati, he even wrote the resolutions asserting that "the authority of the United States, as against the rebellious citizens of the seceding and disloyal States, ought to be maintained, and that whatever men or means may be necessary to accomplish that object the patriotic people of the loyal States will promptly and cheerfully furnish." It did not take long for him to decide he ought to take part in the conflict, for, he mused, he would prefer to go into it if he knew he was to die in the course of it than to live through and after it without taking any part in it.

He was as good as his word. Joining a volunteer company to drill, along with his friend Judge Stanley Matthews, he decided to go into the same regiment, and on June 6 was offered a major's rank while Matthews became a lieutenant colonel. He accepted, and before long, the Twenty-third Ohio Volunteer Infantry was founded, at first under Colonel William S. Rosecrans, but after the latter's promotion to general, under Eliakim P. Scammon, a West Pointer and former professor of mathematics. His strict ways alienated the troops, but Hayes, despite some controversies, managed to establish reasonable relations with him.

The regiment, consisting largely of men from the northern part of the state, was at first somewhat miffed because it had not been able to elect its commanding officer. Hayes succeeded in gaining the regiment's respect very quickly, however. After the troops refused to accept the old flintlock muskets given to them and Scammon ordered the arrest of some of their officers, Hayes, by explaining the situation to the soldiers, managed to calm them and earned their appreciation. He had already written to Lincoln's newly appointed secretary of the Treasury, Salmon P. Chase, whom he knew, asking for arms and money for the regiment.

The unit's duties at Camp Jackson were not onerous. Hayes was delighted to visit with his deceased sister's family in nearby Columbus, where his wife joined him. She had written him for some days that she would love to go with him, and he would soon find that she was fit to be a soldier's wife. "[S]o far it is great fun," he wrote to his friend Manning F. Force. "I enjoy it as much as a boy does the Fourth of July." Much to his wife's gratification, he arranged to have his brother-in-law, Dr. Joseph T. Webb, appointed regimental surgeon and began to learn the routine of army life. On the Fourth of July, he and Matthews formed the regiment into a hollow square and Hayes read the Declaration of Independence and delivered a short speech. Then the men were dismissed. He thought the day was like a Sunday, with fireworks at night. And when the regiment was reviewed by Governor William Dennison and General John C. Frémont, whom he had met the previous evening, the controversial commander impressed him most favorably. "He is a hero," Hayes wrote. "All his words and acts inspire enthusiasm and confidence."

The pleasant stay at Camp Chase did not last long. Toward the end of July, the regiment was ordered to move into what was soon to become West Virginia, to guard the Baltimore and Ohio Railroad, secure the Kanawha Valley, and support the Unionists in the area. By way of Bellaire, the regiment reached Clarksburg, where the Unionists welcomed it with great joy. From there, it advanced to Weston, a beautiful mountain town some twenty-five miles farther south, engaging in little more than occasional clashes with guerrillas. Long marches in the rain, to Buckhannon, Tygart's Valley, Bulltown, French Creek, Summersville, and Sutton were wearying but not particularly eventful. But as Russell H. Conwell, one of Hayes's campaign biographers, pointed out, being detailed to West Virginia was fortuitous for Hayes. While not one of the major battlefields of the war, it was considered the first line of defense for Ohioans, who were naturally interested in these operations and paid close attention to them and the officers and men involved.

On September 10, Hayes experienced his first significant engagement on the Gauley River at Carnifex Ferry near Summersville. The enemy forces now consisted of the combined units of former Secretary of War John B. Floyd and Henry Wise, jointly commanded by Robert E. Lee. Rosecrans, anxious to dislodge those of Floyd, which were strongly entrenched on a hill, after marching seventeen and a half miles, attacked with three brigades. Colonel Scammon's Third Brigade was in reserve until at 4 P.M. it was called to form a line of battle, with the Twenty-third Ohio in front. Ordered to make an independent movement with four companies, Hayes advanced toward the Confederates' works. He climbed up a steep hillside until he reached a high bluff overlooking the Gauley River. Told to use his own judgment, he marched up and down the forbidding inclines, engaging the enemy and suffering a few casualties. Although he still received orders to move forward at dusk, when darkness set in he was finally told to withdraw. On the next day, the Confederates, who had crossed the Gauley River and then destroyed the bridge, were gone. His feelings, Hayes mused, were no different from those he felt at the beginning of an important lawsuit, but he must have enjoyed Rosecrans complimenting him.

Certain aspects of military life were painful to Hayes. When by the colonel's order three youngsters were drummed out of Captain J. L. Drake's company, it made him sick, even though the company approved and the culprits were thieves. And when he had to send a soldier who had stolen a turkey to the guardhouse over Christmas, he hated to do it. A foe of cruelty, he always treated prisoners kindly and was civil to known secessionists.

On September 20, Hayes, who had already tried a number of cases, was ordered to be judge advocate and was attached to headquarters, in the camp of General Jacob Dolson Cox, whom he liked very much. Although the position of judge advocate for the Department of the Ohio entitled him to a higher salary, he was not pleased with his separation from his regiment. But trying case after case, and going from camp to camp, though continuing to complain about his absence from the Twenty-third, he finally considered his duties great fun.

While in the army, Hayes never lost his interest in politics. When his wife complained about Lincoln's reversal of General Frémont's order freeing the slaves in his department—she thought the president lacked decision—he corrected her. Generally optimistic, he assured her that though Lincoln was perhaps not all that could be wished, he was "honest, patriotic, cool-headed, and safe." He did not know of any man who the nation could say was, under all circumstances, to be preferred in his place. His judgment was again more farsighted than that of many of his contemporaries.

His optimism was remarkable. In spite of his initial doubts at Carnifex, he thought the enemy was heartily sick and tired of "this whole business," and only needed a good excuse to give it up. By November, he characterized the enemy officers as more moderate than earlier and, once beaten, glad to have peace so that the old Union could be restored. In December he was sure the enemy was disheartened, and that if England did not interfere and no disaster befell the Union troops, "beyond doubt" the rebels would be conquered at no distant period. Entertaining these views, he was sure that the rebellion would be crushed rapidly. Evidence to the contrary apparently did not bother him.

His dissatisfaction with his separation from his regiment was soon resolved. Promoted on October 23 to lieutenant colonel to take the place of his friend Matthews, who became colonel of the Fifty-fourth Ohio Regiment, he was relieved from judicial duty and returned to the Twenty-third. Pleased to be called colonel rather than major, he now had to learn the duties of the higher rank and, as he put it, see that Colonel Scammon did not forget or omit anything. The regiment was then stationed at Camp Tompkins near Gauley Bridge. The enemy was at the opposite side of the New River, with the Gauley one of the two streams forming the Kanawha, leaving the Twenty-third just outside the range of enemy shells. Pursuing General Floyd's forces but delayed by high water, the regiment arrived at the largely deserted pleasant village of Fayetteville, where it prepared for winter quarters.

Because Lucy was expecting again, Hayes was doubly anxious for news from home. On December 23, to his delight, she had another son, Joe, and he planned a leave to go home. But because Major J. M. Comly, with five companies, including two of the Twenty-third, had been sent to Raleigh, twenty-five miles to the south, Hayes had to stay a while longer. He remained in Fayetteville, where he had already welcomed the many "contrabands"— enemy slaves—who surrendered to him. Considering them free, he sent them on to Ohio. Then, at the beginning of the new year, he too went to Raleigh, to Camp Hayes, as Comly had called his encampment. Encounters with bushwhackers kept him busy until, in February 1862, the leave finally came through. He could go home to see his newborn son and visit family, friends, and relatives.

When he returned, by rail, hack, and steamship, first to Camp Piatt near Charleston, then to Fayetteville, and then to Raleigh, rain and snow were besetting the troops in West Virginia's inhospitable mountains. But Hayes was pleased that he was now in General Frémont's command, although he was no longer so convinced that the end of the war was near. Slavery would have to be abolished in the seceded states, he argued, while the border states ought to be allowed to solve the matter by themselves. It was the policy eventually adopted by the government, and he noted with approval that President Lincoln had already called on the border states to end the institution. The rest of Hayes's prescription would follow.

On April 11, the news of the capture of Island No. 10 on the Mississippi and the result of the Battle of Shiloh restored his optimism. He was convinced again that the rebellion was waning, even though Shiloh did not prove as decisive as he had hoped.

That April, the regiment, part of General Cox's division of three brigades, was to move south once more. Cox intended to proceed toward Princeton and the railroad to Tennessee at Wytheville and Dublin. Because of the importance of the line, Hayes expected heavy resistance; the move was delayed by steady rains, and after leaving Raleigh, it was not until the end of the month that the regiment finally reached the foot of Flattop Mountain on the line between Raleigh and Mercer counties. On May 1, now part of the command of Colonel (soon to be General) George Crook, a capable West Pointer who had seen Indian fighting in the Northwest, Hayes managed to rout a small party of the enemy. The graycoats, commanded by Colonel Walter H. Jenifer, had seriously menaced Lt. J. L. Botsford, whom Hayes had sent ahead to Clark's Hollow. He not only relieved Botsford at Camp Creek but also drove Jenifer all the way through Princeton, which the Confederates burned. His actions earned the special commendation of General J. D. Cox, who added his own "express satisfaction at the promptness of Lieutenant-Colonel Hayes in marching upon Princeton" to Frémont's general commendation of the troops. Yet in spite of this success, Scammon censured Hayes for having been too far forward, a criticism the lieutenant colonel deeply resented. The affair deserved praise, not censure, he replied.

From Princeton, Hayes moved to Pearisburg, where, after capturing stores and some prisoners, he was attacked by four thousand Confederates under General Henry Heth. After destroying the captured stores, Hayes, slightly wounded by a piece of ball, "retreated in excellent order," as Scammon reported, and returned to a camp north of the East River near the present state line between West Virginia and Virginia. Lucy, who had heard the Confederates had taken Princeton, was relieved that Rud and Joe were all right and that the wound was "a mere scratch." A difficult retreat to Princeton followed.

The regiment's next headquarters was at Flattop Mountain, where his daily activities were not taxing. Breakfast started at five; then there was some respite, then a visit to Colonel Scammon's brigade headquarters, then to General Jacob D. Cox's division headquarters, where the assembled officers discussed politics, then a return to the regiment, and reading till dinner. In the afternoon he enjoyed some horseback riding. Then more reading, largely novels until the arrival of the telegraphic news and the mails at five, and finally "gossip" and newspaper reading till bedtime at nine. The long-promised rifled muskets also finally arrived. They were old, their accuracy left much to be desired, but their power was beyond question.

Lucy and the children had gone to Chillicothe to stay with her relatives. In a letter to Hayes she expressed her disappointment with President Lincoln's placing General John Pope in charge of all the Mountain Department and the Valley, thus causing the resignation of her hero Frémont, who she thought had shown true bravery. She contrasted Lincoln's vacillation about Frémont with the firmness with which he sustained McClellan. And, she added, the "protection of slavery is costing us many precious lives." While sympathizing with her, her husband did not join in the attack on the president. He thought that recent disasters—McClellan's failure before Richmond—might lead to the abolition of slavery and thus do some good.

On July 12 Scammon ordered Hayes to move with six companies of the Twenty-third to Green Meadows. As it was lower than Flattop Mountain, it was hot and uncomfortable. Hayes was in command not merely of the six companies of the Twenty-third, but also of some cavalry, a squad of a battery, and a squad of the Second Union Virginia. Raiding into the enemy's lines, his soldiers captured horses, cattle, and prisoners. On July 23, Hayes was promoted to colonel—but of the Seventy-ninth, not the Twenty-third regiment. Having become attached to his unit, he was hesitant about accepting. On August 6, hearing that pickets on New River above Blue Stone had been cut off, Hayes sent two companies there to investigate. Before these companies could return, it was rumored that four thousand enemy troops had passed down the river on the other side to attack the ferry. Hayes, who soon found there were many fewer opponents, sent reinforcements, had the band play loudly, and the enemy withdrew.

Before he could decide on his promotion, he was ordered east to join Pope's Army of Virginia. By way of Washington, the troops were sent to a camp in Maryland fifteen miles north of the capital. Their colonel made himself again popular by standing up to General Marcus A. Reno, who had chastised them in derisive language about taking straw from a stack for a bedding on the floor. The troops had always done so, Hayes said, and if necessary, they would pay for the straw. Adding that he hoped the generals would show as much energy in dealing with their foes as they did with their friends, he infuriated Reno, especially as his troops cheered him, and the commanding general threatened to put him in chains.

After Pope's defeat at the Second Bull Run, Lincoln recalled McClellan, and Hayes's regiment took part in the preliminaries of the Battle of Antietam. At South Mountain near Sharpsburg, General Cox's division formed the vanguard of Ambrose Burnside's army, with the Twenty-third in front. Ordered to attack the Confederates at the crest of the mountain at the crossing of the old national road, Hayes pushed the enemy into the woods, then engaged a force coming from a neighboring hill and drove it out of the thicket. As he commanded a third charge, he was struck above the elbow. Major James M. Comly, whose skill he had long admired, took over command, although Hayes rallied, and with a handkerchief tied around his arm began to lead again. But the wound was too severe. He lay down, and when the firing lessened, called out, "Hallo, Twenty-third men, are you going to leave your colonel here for the enemy?" Half a dozen soldiers immediately appeared, offering to take him back; as the enemy opened fire on them, however, he ordered them back to cover. Then one of his lieutenants finally led him to the rear.

The wound was dangerous. His brother-in-law, Dr. Joe, who dressed it, despaired of his recovery; nevertheless he was able to walk half a mile to a neighboring house, from where he was driven by ambulance to nearby Middletown. A friendly local family took him in, provided excellent care, and his arm gradually got better.

In the meantime, Lucy had heard only rumors, some insisting that her husband had been killed. Not knowing where he was, she went to Washington, together with William A. Platt, his brother-in-law, and finally met some soldiers of the Twenty-third, who directed her to Middletown. Husband and wife were naturally delighted to be reunited, and Lucy not only took care of her spouse but also looked after the wounded soldiers in the neighborhood. Scammon was finally satisfied. "I was very sorry to hear of your wound," he wrote. "Take care of yourself and get well as soon as you can. Our Brigade and Division did splendidly; we can say this between ourselves." General Cox also sent his regards.

On September 22, Abraham Lincoln issued his Preliminary Emancipation Proclamation freeing all slaves in rebellious territory after January 1, 1863. And while Lucy had again expressed the most bitter feelings about the president after the disaster at the

Second Bull Run, her husband, more politically astute, and always friendlier to Lincoln, wrote that he was not sure about the proclamation, but that he was content. Democratic gains in the November elections did not worry him. He hoped that they would only spur the administration to more vigor. He expressed his satisfaction at the dismissal of McClellan and the trial of Don Carlos Buell and Fitz-John Porter, as well as his appreciation of Ambrose E. Burnside and Rosecrans. The Battle of Fredericksburg lessened his regard for the former, who, he thought, might have to yield to McClellan. Nevertheless, he was hopeful. "We now have the Emancipation Proclamation to go upon," he wrote. " Will not this stiffen the President's backbone so as to drive it through?"

On October 24, Hayes, who had not yet accepted his previous promotion, finally became a full colonel and, Scammon having been promoted and sent to Point Pleasant, was able to take over command of the Twenty-third. He withdrew the discharge he had obtained in order to take command of the Seventy-ninth regiment, and after his recovery returned to his regiment, now once again in West Virginia at Gauley Bridge. Soon appointed officer in chief of the First Brigade, Second Kanawha Division, he was asked to act as brigadier general. His hesitation about the Seventy-ninth had paid off.

He was delighted to be back. It felt like coming home. As a good commander, he enjoyed meeting his old troops again, and he knew his men. When on December 13 the newly appointed second lieutenant William McKinley, the future president of the United States, rejoined the regiment, Hayes characterized him as "an exceedingly bright, intelligent, and gentlemanly young officer" who promised to be "one of our best." He would become ever more friendly with McKinley as time went on, and eventually appointed him his quartermaster.

Early in the New Year, Hayes for a few months enjoyed comparative quiet. Lucy and the two oldest boys came to visit him again and the whole family enjoyed camp life. They returned home in

March, when the brigade moved to Camp White opposite Charleston.

As usual, Hayes's political views at this time were moderate. He did not expect a great deal from the newly promulgated Emancipation Proclamation but did affirm he was glad it was issued. And he felt that the Democrats, when in power, would soon become a good enough war party and even become abolitionists. His optimism had not been dimmed by the ever-lengthening nature of the conflict.

Hayes was not inactive at Camp White. At the end of March, he achieved a minor success in a skirmish at Point Pleasant; twenty rebels were killed and fifty taken prisoner. General Albert G. Jenkins cut off the Federals for four days, but then Hayes's command succeeded in repelling two of the Confederate assaults. As Camp White was well fortified, secure against any but major attacks, on June 14 his entire family, wife, children, and mother, came to the encampment to be with him. After a few days' happiness, however, his youngest boy, little Joe, died of dysentery. He had seen so little of him that he was less affected than might have been expected, but the loss was hard for the mother and grandmother, who left on July 1. Lucy would return in September.

Hardly had the family left than the regiment also decamped, sailing up the Kanawha River to Camp Joe Webb, near Fayetteville. An expedition to Raleigh City followed, though Hayes thought his forces were too weak to accomplish anything. When he reached Raleigh on July 14, he found the enemy too strong for assault; yet the next morning the Confederates had gone.

Upon his return to Fayetteville, Hayes heard that John Hunt Morgan, the Confederate raider, had invaded Ohio. After some argument, he convinced Scammon to send three regiments, including the Twenty-third, to Gallipolis. On arriving there by boat, Hayes learned that the raider had pushed up the Ohio River in order to try crossing at Pomeroy, and he followed. Morgan arrived; together with the Thirteenth and the Twenty-third, Hayes, inflicting some losses, drove him off. But his failure to pursue and catch

Morgan, according to the historian T. Harry Williams, was his worst mistake during the war. On July 20, Morgan was at Buffington Island, where the Twenty-third and General Henry M. Judah's cavalry also dispersed him. His raids in Ohio were over. Back at Camp White, Hayes, unmindful of future criticism, looked back on the campaign as the liveliest and jolliest he had ever been in. Morgan's threat to the Buckeye State had been dispelled.

But Rud's optimism was not dimmed. It is not surprising that the great victories at Gettysburg and Vicksburg encouraged him. "All things look very well," he wrote. "The escape of Lee does not disappoint me. To get rid of him so easily is a success. We shall get him someday." Morgan's raid into Ohio he considered proof of the enemy's "despairing and lost cause." Even the bad news of Rosecrans's defeat at Chickamauga did not change his conviction of ultimate victory. "We shall recover from the blow," he mused. And then came the victory of Union candidate John Brough over the notorious Copperhead Clement C. Vallandigham in the Ohio gubernatorial election in October. Hayes thought it equal to a triumph of arms in an important battle.

In view of the fact that their three years' enlistment was about to expire, Hayes tried to urge his troops to reenlist. Partially successful, he was able to persuade a great number to do so. In Company B of the Twenty-third alone, 75 percent reenlisted. A leave was the result, and at the end of November he went to Gallipolis to meet the family.

In the beginning of December, the colonel took part in a short campaign to cooperate with General William W. Averell in an attack on the railroad at Salem, Virginia. After successfully reaching Lewisburg, Scammon, hearing of enemy reinforcements, ordered a retreat. Hayes commented that it was "a good trip for the season."

Early in February 1864 General Scammon was captured, a mishap Hayes found amusing, because the general was known for his caution and had bored fellow officers with his constant talk of vigilance. He who thought the greatest crime was to be surprised was now a victim himself, though he was eventually exchanged.

After a pleasant leave in Ohio, and another visit by Lucy, who finally settled down in Chillicothe, Hayes set out on his spring campaign. As commander of the First Brigade of infantry, consisting of four regiments, he served under General George Crook, the able commander called "Uncle George" by the troops, who was about to engage in a raid upon the Virginia and Tennessee Railroad. He reached his target, but before he could set fire to the New River Bridge, his objective, he had to engage in the bloody Battle of Cloyd's Mountain. The First Brigade, ordered to the left to form at the edge of a wood, charged over a meadow a quarter- to a half-mile wide; the Twenty-third and the Thirty-sixth Ohio sprang into a ditch and up a steep wooded hill, where the rebel breastworks were located. With heavy casualties, a loss of 250 men, Hayes rushed on; the bluecoats carried the position, captured some 300 prisoners, among them General Albert G. Jenkins, five pieces of artillery and many stores, and entered Dublin. On May 10, in spite of rebel resistance, they burned the bridge. Then they moved on to Blackburg, destroying eighteen miles of the railroad as they went. Encountering General William L. "Mudsill" Jackson and 1,500 men, they completely routed his army.

But the aftermath was less glorious. Crook, without news for days, now feared he was going to be cut off and ordered a retreat. It was a difficult trip through rain-soaked roads, little food, and lack of ferryboats. One small boat had to accommodate the army, and horses and mules had to swim. General Crook himself took a hand in forcing mules into the river. Nevertheless, back in West Virginia at Meadow Bluff, Hayes thought the twenty-one-day campaign was the most successful and pleasant he had ever had. Crook commended Hayes among the other brigade commanders for their "personal bravery, their hearty cooperation, and the intelligent manner" in which they carried out and anticipated his orders and plans.

At the beginning of June, Hayes and his brigade moved into the Valley of Virginia. Engaging rebel troops and destroying the railroad along the way, they reached Staunton, recently captured by General

David Hunter. On June 11, after a three hour sharpshooters' and artillery fight, with Hayes's brigade in the lead, Hunter's army, of which Crook's formed a part, captured Lexington. From Staunton, Crook with Hayes's brigade was sent to reach the rear of Lynchburg, again tearing up railroads, but Hunter recalled them when Confederate reinforcements reached the city, and the brigade returned to West Virginia.

Back at Camp Elk near Charleston, Hayes was happy about the new command of General Crook, of whom he was very fond, while both he and the troops disliked Hunter, who was too radical to be popular. Crook had received an independent command in the department of West Virginia, styled the Army of the Kanawha, of which the First Brigade and the Twenty-third was part. The arrangement fully served Hayes's purposes.

In the middle of July, the brigade was ordered to Martinsburg. From there Crook's army moved to Winchester, where General Jubal A. Early's superior Confederate forces inflicted a serious reverse on the bluecoats. Hayes, who lost his horse during the battle, expertly covered the unit's retreat. His campaign biographer, J. Q. Howard, maintained that he saved the command from annihilation.

On August 7, Philip H. Sheridan took command of the Middle Military Division to start his Shenandoah Valley campaign. Crook's forces joined him, and Hayes took part in the final destruction of the Confederate forces in the area.

The Shenandoah Valley campaign was not easy. There were frequent skirmishes and firefights, with Hayes in advance, first at Halltown, then at Berryville, then at Winchester, where Crook's corps, originally in reserve, managed to contribute to the final victory. At this third battle of Winchester, on September 19, "General Crook's command in general, and my brigade and the second Kanawha Division in particular," as Hayes wrote, squared up the balance of the earlier defeat. At first the Federals were driven back, but then, with Hayes in front, Crook successfully counterattacked. While crossing Opequon Creek, Hayes lost his horse, went on foot through the water and emerged on the other side. Initially, he found himself alone, but then other units crossed the stream and the bluecoats achieved a great victory. He was extremely proud of his feat. Three days later, Crook's forces were once more part of Sheridan's success at Fisher's Hill, where Early had entrenched on a steep mountain near Strasburg. Crook's Corps ascended the mountain from the right flank with Hayes in advance, and Early was again defeated.

On October 18, Early, who had steadily moved southward, attempted to fall upon the Union flank and rear at Cedar Creek. At first he succeeded, and Hayes, with some fourteen hundred effectives, attempted to lead these calmly toward the rear. When his horse was shot, he was thrown off, hurting his ankle and foot, but he rallied and brought the retreat to a standstill. Then, after his famous ride, Sheridan arrived. The tide turned and the day ended in a great victory.

The Valley campaign was not the only contest that summer and fall. Abraham Lincoln had been renominated and was opposed by General McClellan, who had become the Democratic candidate on a peace platform, which he repudiated. Hayes supported the president; he even chided his wife for criticizing Lincoln for failing to protect Union prisoners by retaliation, a measure he was too humane to sanction. But he was strangely indifferent to the struggle. If McClellan were nominated, he wrote, he would be satisfied, as the Democratic party would become a war party. When the general did become the opposition candidate, Rud reflected that he was not bad, only in bad company, and he appreciated the letter rejecting the peace platform. But he believed Lincoln would win. As a Republican, he naturally voted for him in November. The president's victory would hasten the end of the war.

Hayes himself was also up for election. On August 6, the 2nd congressional district of Cincinnati nominated him for a seat in the House of Representatives. "You have been chosen to represent the loyal sentiments of this district, from a conviction that courage, ability, and singlehearted devotion to the country are qualities as necessary in the legislative assembly as on the battlefield," the president of the convention informed him. While consenting, Hayes refused to take a furlough and campaign, although his friend William Henry Smith, a journalist and secretary of state of Ohio, urged him to do so, only to receive a decisive declination. "An officer fit for duty who at this crisis would abandon his post to electioneer for a seat in Congress ought to be scalped," Hayes wrote. "You may feel perfectly sure I shall do no such thing." Thus the campaign went on without the candidate, and when the Democrats, with the banker Joseph C. Butler as their candidate, displayed a banner showing Hayes dodging bullets, indignant veterans charged them, and the banner was removed. His stance served him well, so that he was elected on October 11. He would not have to take office until December 1865.

After Cedar Creek, Hayes went into camp near Winchester. His brigade could rest for a change, while he himself earned the reward for his actions. On November 30, upon recommendations by Generals Sheridan and Crook, he was appointed brigadier general "for gallant and meritorious service in the battles of Opequon, Fisher's Hill, and Middletown, Virginia." His rank, to date from October 19, finally matched his duties as brigade commander, and he was delighted with the new shoulder straps General Crook gave him.

On January 10, 1865, from his headquarters in Camp Hastings near Cumberland, Maryland, the new general went home for a month's leave to see his new son, George Crook, born in October. His wife visited him upon his return to Camp Hastings, but fell ill and went home again. Then General Crook was captured, a misfortune Hayes termed a "disaster." Winfield Scott Hancock took over, but the war was rapidly drawing to a close. Hayes, who on March 13 was brevetted major general "for distinguished and gallant services in the Campaign of 1864," decided to go home as soon as Richmond was taken. Still, on April 5, he received a new command of cavalry, infantry, and artillery, at New Creek, West Virginia, which he was to lead over the mountains to Lynchburg. Considering this task difficult, he was soon relieved by Lee's surrender, which rendered the whole project superfluous. "I wonder if you feel as happy as I do," he wrote to Lucy.

Lincoln's assassination soon dampened Hayes's elation. "When I heard first yesterday morning of the awful tragedy at Washington," he wrote to Lucy, "I was pained and shocked to a degree I have never before experienced. . . . The probable consequences, or rather the possible results in their worst imaginable form, were presented to my mind one after the other, until I really began to feel that there was a calamity so extensive that in no direction could be found any, the slightest, glimmer of consolation." Deeply disturbed, he considered the tragedy a great loss for the country. But he thought it was fortunate that it had not occurred earlier. Realizing that Lincoln's fame was secure, he saw that the martyred president was "the darling of History evermore" and that his life and achievements gave him "titles to regard second to those of no other man in ancient or modern times."

It did not take long for Hayes to regain his happiness about the final Union victory. Regarding Joseph E. Johnston's surrender as the end of the war, he delightedly wore a white collar for the first time since 1861. Late in April, he obtained a leave to go to Washington, where he stayed with his friend Judge William Johnston, who had urged him to come for some time. He met the new president, Andrew Johnson, and was more favorably impressed than he had anticipated. He would soon change his mind.

Upon his return to New Creek, Hayes sent in his resignation from the army, which was accepted on June 8. Lucy arrived, and the two took another trip to Washington and also to Richmond before returning to Ohio.

Thus ended Hayes's wartime career. He had performed very well, shown considerable bravery, and contributed materially to the victories at Cloyd's Mountain and Winchester. It was a record of which he could justly be proud, and ever after he looked back upon it with great satisfaction.

# 3

---

# Congressman and Governor

Hayes's election to the House while still in the field in the fall of 1864 did not interfere with his command as he did not have to take his seat until December 1865. By that time he had resigned from the army so that he had no difficulty in appearing at the meeting of the new Congress. A good Republican, he had already taken part in the successful campaign to elect General Jacob Dolson Cox governor of Ohio. In Congress, he supported his party's measures from the first, although he did not consider himself a radical of the type of Thaddeus Stevens, the determined leader of the extremist faction of the party and chairman of the House Ways and Means Committee.

Before he could go to the capital, he had to reorder his domestic arrangements. As his apartment in Cincinnati was not yet available, Lucy went to Chillicothe without him, while he moved into a room at Fourth and Walnut Streets. It was not until October that his old home was ready and the family could really be reunited, at least for a short time. At the end of November, he had to leave Lucy again to take his seat. He went to Washington and took an apartment at 452 Thirteenth Street. Although he had not been too anxious to enter Congress, the perquisites of the members pleased him. They were entitled to all the back numbers of the *Congressional Globe*, a small library, seventy dollars for stationery, fifty dollars for newspapers, and twenty-four copies of the current *Globe*.

His congressional work started at once. On December 1, he attended a caucus of Union members who decided not to admit any Southern delegates, even those undoubtedly loyal, to support Edward McPherson for Clerk, and Schuyler Colfax for Speaker of the House. A second caucus on the next day, in which he also took part, confirmed the previous selections. At this conclave Thaddeus Stevens succeeded in calling for a Joint Committee of Fifteen on Reconstruction, to which all matters pertaining to the South were to be referred. After these preliminaries, on December 4, the House was organized according to the Republican arrangements. That Stevens was the evident leader of the body was clear to Hayes, who characterized him as "grim-looking, cool with a ready wit, perfect courage, and the sort of independence which long experience, assured position, and seventy years of age give any able man." He himself was made chairman of the Joint Committee on the Library, a "no-account committee in the public sense," as he characterized it, though he had long been an avid reader interested in books. He also became a member of the Committee on Public Lands.

The new Congress soon challenged President Johnson, who had attempted to confront it with a fait accompli by trying to restore the seceded states during the recess. Acting on his conviction that the states were still in the Union, he had offered them an easy way of "restoration," as he called it. By accepting an amnesty for all but fourteen exempted classes, they could reestablish their governments by merely taking an oath of loyalty and abolishing slavery. Although he also suggested that they nullify the secession ordinances and repudiate the Confederate debt, he did not even insist on these terms. The result was the establishment of extremely conservative administrations. Most Southern states passed vicious "black codes" attempting to reduce the freedmen once again to a level close to slavery, none enfranchised any blacks, and many elected prominent ex-Confederates to Congress, including the ex-vice president of the Confederacy. Not surprisingly, Congress denied seats to these archconservatives, thus making it clear that it would not recognize the Johnson regimes. Supporting this policy as well as the other measures advocated by the Republican majority, Hayes proved himself a loyal party member. After all, the Republicans could hardly be indifferent to the South's gaining representation in Congress by the lapse of the constitutional clause counting slaves as three-fifths of a person, to say nothing of the likelihood of the former Confederates electing enough Democrats to take over both houses. However, he was never an extreme radical and maintained excellent relations with his Confederate friend Guy Bryan and other Southerners. Like many other Republicans he believed that the Southern states had forfeited their rights and ought to be reconstructed by Congress, but unlike Stevens did not feel that they were conquered provinces and were thus no longer covered by the Constitution.

Late in January, Lucy arrived to spend a happy month with her husband. Visiting the House gallery every day, she apparently enjoyed the proceedings. The capital's social life seemed less agreeable. The couple avoided receptions as much as possible; Hayes felt these were all alike and bored him, although he did attend two parties given by General Grant and Secretary of the Interior James Harlan.

Like many Republican members of Congress, for some time Hayes continued to hope that a break with Johnson might be avoided. But the president was adamant. Instead of coming to some understanding with at least the moderate Republicans, on February 19 he vetoed the Freedmen's Bureau Bill, designed to renew and strengthen a measure passed in Lincoln's administration to assist freedmen and prepared by the moderate Senator Lyman Trumbull. To make matters worse, three days later he delivered a speech comparing the radical leaders to Jefferson Davis. Yet as late as February 28, Hayes still expressed a faint hope that Johnson might return "to the bosom of his family." Should the president sign the civil rights measure, containing many of the provisions of the later Fourteenth Amendment, and sign the bill for the admission of Tennessee, he thought everything might still be all right. But when Johnson vetoed the Civil Rights Bill, Hayes, like most other Republicans, gave up his hopes of reconciliation. Voting to override the veto, Hayes thereafter strongly opposed Johnson, who, he felt, had fallen completely under the influence of former rebels. Thus he freely supported the Fourteenth Amendment extending civil rights to blacks, authorizing a reduction in representation for any state denying the vote to males over twenty-one years of age, and merely disfranchising those insurgents who had formerly held federal positions. Having long thought that the South could not be readmitted until the amendment was safe, he favored it even though it did not confer suffrage on the freedmen, who, he believed, were citizens and ought to obtain the vote, by federal action in the former Confederacy and the territories and by state action elsewhere. But unlike the extreme radicals, he also felt that education—the ability to read and write—ought to be a prerequisite for the ballot. The president, on the other hand, opposing the amendment, continued to insist that the right of suffrage was a matter for the states to decide.

His satisfaction about the radical successes, particularly the overriding of the Civil Rights Bill veto, which he celebrated at a party given by General Grant, was clouded by a personal tragedy. In May his little boy George died of scarlet fever. Hayes had gone back to Ohio to be with the family when the child fell ill, but thinking he was better, returned to Washington only to find out that the boy had passed away. It was a hard blow, and his separation from Lucy did not make it any easier. Whether he tried to forget or whether he merely wanted a change, in July he visited the battlefield at Gettysburg, but then, because of the extended session of Congress, was retained in Washington somewhat longer. The lawmakers repassed a new version of the Freedmen's Bureau Bill over the president's veto, as well as a measure for the readmission of Tennessee, the only state that had ratified the amendment.

In August, the important midterm campaign for a new Congress started. At stake were the efforts of Johnson to defeat the congressional plan of Reconstruction, particularly the Fourteenth Amendment. Unlike in other such contests, four national conventions were held. Renominated without opposition on August 4, Hayes took an active part in the campaign. He attended the Southern Loyalist Convention in Philadelphia, called to counter Johnson's National Union Convention in the same city, and, to contest the efforts of the opposition, delivered speeches almost every night. The Democrats, relying on racist appeals against the blacks, nominated Thomas Cook, who also had the backing of the Workingman's party, to run against him for his seat in Congress.

He minced no words. There were two plans of Reconstruction, he said in an address in Cincinnati, Lincoln's and Jefferson Davis's, and Johnson's was like the latter. Lincoln restored states to the hands of loyal men while Johnson placed them in the grip of rebel legislatures with their black codes—a situation that could be corrected by the Fourteenth Amendment. His campaigning was successful enough to bring about his reelection, albeit by a reduced majority of about three thousand, but the Democrats carried the legislature. To Guy Bryan, who maintained a Southern point of view, he explained that the congressional plan did not "disfranchise" anybody; it merely disqualified Confederate leaders who had been former officeholders, and even that restriction could be removed by a two-thirds vote of Congress. Thus it did not affect anybody under twenty-seven or twenty-eight, and he pleaded with his friend that it be accepted, as the South would never get any better terms. But of course the South and Johnson remained obdurate.

Before going back to Washington, Hayes traveled to Omaha and the West on a journey sponsored by the Union Pacific Railroad. His friend Ralph Buckland joined him in Chicago, and he enjoyed the interlude. Upon his return home, he was saddened by the loss of his mother, with whom he had been so close as to correspond with great regularity, but, an enthusiastic traveler, shortly after his arrival in the capital he took another trip. Leaving his two oldest boys with his uncle in Fremont, where they went to school, during the Christmas recess he took Ruddy, Lucy, Buckland, and his wife with him to Washington, where he joined a group of radical members of Congress, including Senator Benjamin F. Wade, on a jaunt to New Orleans. Among other places, he visited Charlottesville, Lynchburg, and Knoxville, as well as the battlefields at Chattanooga and elsewhere, and enjoyed meeting rebel officers with whom he established friendly relations. In Memphis, addressing some freedmen in Memphis, he found their eager faces most stimulating.

During his renewed service in Congress, Lucy accompanied him for part of the time. But this office was cut short, as he resigned before the term was up in order to run for governor of Ohio. During that brief time, however, he continued to participate in the Republican battle with the president. Because he was a radical, at least as he called himself, he wrote to his friend W. M. Dickson that he feared he might have lost his "smart" and wanted to hear from a cool outsider. Though he thought the president might be yielding, Johnson, instead of settling on the basis of the amendment, continued to oppose it with all his might. Congress replied with measures designed to fence him in. Over Johnson's veto or objections, it passed a Tenure of Office Act to prevent him from dismissing appointees without the consent of the Senate; command of the army provisions in the Military Appropriations Act of 1867–1868 to curtail his powers as commander in chief of the army, demanding that his orders be transmitted through the General of the Army to be stationed in Washington; and a measure calling the Fortieth Congress into session in March immediately upon the expiration of the Thirty-ninth to keep watch upon him during the spring and summer. In the end, again over his vetoes, Congress passed a series of Reconstruction Acts remanding the Southern states to military rule until they had set up a government based on universal suffrage and ratified the amendment. Hayes supported all of these measures, even abandoning his original preference for suffrage based on education.

In July, he took his sons Birch and Webb with him to Washington. At first they were somewhat subdued, but then they relaxed, and Webb became friendly with the various congressmen aboard the train. Both crowded up to Thad Stevens, whom Birch admired most. When Congress adjourned on July 20, their father went home with the boys and resigned. His service in the House was over.

All in all, his career in Congress had not been particularly remarkable. Speaking rarely, he had made no particular contributions to legislation, but he had won a number of friends. Still, as chairman of the Library Committee, he had gained support for the effort to add two wings to the Library of Congress and for the transfer of the library of the Smithsonian Institution to the former. The committee was also able to obtain appropriations for the purchase of books.

His congressional service had led to his nomination for governor. When early in 1867 Governor Cox declined a renomination, a number of friends, including Comly and William Henry Smith, asked Hayes to seek the office. As usual, at first he was, or pretended to be, doubtful, but hearing that he was most popular and that a candidate with a military record was needed rather than former Congressman Samuel Galloway, the other contender, he finally consented. At any rate, he did not particularly enjoy congressional life and had no ambition for congressional reputation or influence. Executive duties were much more to his liking.

He faced a difficult campaign. Nominated on the second ballot on June 19 at the Republican state convention in Columbus, Hayes was running on a platform endorsing a constitutional amendment mandating impartial manhood suffrage in Ohio. This plank, conferring the right to vote on African Americans, was most unpopular in a state that had long discriminated against blacks, and the Democrats made the most of it. Girls dressed in white carried signs,

"Fathers save us from negro equality," and their chances of success increased day by day. His opponent, Allen G. Thurman, a peace Democrat and former chief justice of Ohio whose reputation as a lawyer was unexcelled, constantly inveighed against the amendment. According to Daniel Porter, only three newspapers supported the change, while three others, opposing the amendment, gave Hayes but questionable support, although he could rely on the loyalty of the veterans. Delivering speeches in place after place, eighty-one to Thurman's seventy-one, Hayes sought to counteract these tactics with the reply, "Honest colored men are preferable to white traitors." And he waved the bloody shirt. At Lebanon on August 5 he accused the Democrats of still using the states' rights theory with which they had excused slavery; their plan for Reconstruction was based on the same idea, while the Republicans made the blacks citizens as they had been in 1776. He added, "Permeated and sustained by a conviction that, in this contest the Union party of Ohio is doing battle for the right, I enter upon my part of the labors of the canvass with undoubting confidence that the goodness of the cause will make up for the weakness of its advocacy." Turning to the financial issue, in Batavia he criticized his opponent for wanting to pay government bonds in greenbacks, an idea he had always opposed. He was an unwavering supporter of conservative money policies, the immutability of a gold currency, a question that recurred in Sidney, where he also raised the Reconstruction issue again, denigrating the advocacy of states' rights and praising the supremacy of the national government.

The campaign ended badly. In spite of efforts of visiting radicals like Zachariah Chandler, the Democrats defeated the amendment and captured the legislature, which was to cast ballots for a senator in place of Benjamin F. Wade. They also elected their candidate, Samuel F. Carey, to Hayes's vacant seat in Congress. Hayes, who originally had thought himself beaten, scraped through by the narrowest of margins, a three thousand majority, a victory that made him governor with a hostile legislature. According to Eugene H. Roseboom, this result was not too disadvantageous, as his lack of a veto power rendered him immune from criticism of laws passed by the assembly.

In the meantime, Lucy had given birth to a girl, whom her parents called Fanny after Hayes's beloved sister. The family now consisted of three boys, Birch, Webb, Ruddy, and the little girl, a matter of great joy to their parents. The eldest, Birch, was a bright boy fond of learning, who eventually went to Cornell, studied law, and became an attorney. Webb, the second, was less fond of learning but became his father's assistant, and Ruddy, the youngest, who had bad eyesight and was somewhat sickly, stayed at home while his older brothers were away at school. Eventually he attended an agricultural college in Michigan and then turned to banking. After obtaining a pleasant house in Columbus, Hayes made preparations to welcome Lucy and the family to the state capital.

Hayes was inaugurated on January 13, 1868. In his inaugural address, he praised his predecessor, Governor Cox. Expressing his satisfaction with the condition of the state's finances, he warned against excessive legislation, called again for impartial suffrage, and protested against any repeal of the ratification of the Fourteenth Amendment. The address was the shortest inaugural ever to have been delivered in Ohio.

The powers of the governors of Ohio were extremely limited. Denied the right to veto legislation, they found their time and correspondence largely taken up with appointments of judges, boards of trustees and directors of charitable institutions, colleges, and universities, the granting or denial of pardons to convicts, and the extradition of criminals. Under these circumstances, Hayes did not find his new job burdensome. "I am enjoying the new office," he wrote to his uncle. "It strikes me at a guess as the pleasantest I have ever had. Not too much hard work—plenty of time to read—good society &c &c." He did what he could to facilitate the completion of a new asylum for the deaf and dumb, advocated the establishment of a reform school for girls, tried to acquire as many portraits of former governors as possible to be placed in the state house, and took steps to prevent the spread of rinderpest in livestock. But his plea against the attempted repeal of the ratification of the Fourteenth Amendment fell on deaf ears. On January 15, the legislature passed a resolution reversing its predecessors, although the secretary of state refused to recognize the validity of the effort.

Of course, Hayes continued to take part in national politics. In February 1868 the House of Representatives finally impeached Johnson, whom the radicals had charged with violation of the Tenure of Office Act and failure to carry out their Reconstruction program. A sensational trial followed, with most Republicans favoring the president's conviction. Hayes, strongly supporting the impeachment, was in full accord with his party. When asked what Ohio Republicans desired, he answered with one word, "Conviction." The Senate acquitted the president by one vote, but by that time Hayes was already engaged in the nomination and election campaign for General Grant. Attending the national convention in Chicago, which nominated the general, he was accompanied by young Mrs. Benjamin F. Wade, whose senator husband had hopes of securing the vice presidential nomination. Wade's failure to obtain it was the only exception to a meeting that otherwise Hayes called a great success.

He plunged immediately into the campaign. Worried about the defection of the Jews because of Grant's 1862 order expelling them from the Department of the Tennessee, he sought ways of winning them back. He delivered campaign speeches all over the state, at Lawrence, Urbana, Ironton, Marietta, and Portsmouth, among other places, and cosponsored a mass meeting with the participation of veterans in Cleveland. The Democrats' nomination of Horatio Seymour, the Civil War governor of New York, and Francis Blair, ex-Republican but now a determined foe of Reconstruction, encouraged him—"a wet blanket here to our Democrats," he called the ticket. A Republican victory in Indiana seemed to assure national success, especially when a splendid outcome in Ohio followed, and in November Grant was elected president. Delighted at the result, Hayes visited the general immediately afterward. He found his host sensible, clear-headed, and well informed, and feeling completely at ease with Grant, he expressed his conviction that the incoming administration would be most successful. At the same time, he procured a pardon for their Confederate activities for Guy Bryan and his brother from President Johnson.

On November 23, he delivered his first annual message to the legislature. Recommending a revision of the tax laws as advocated by a previous commission, he also asked the legislature for funds for the rebuilding of the lunatic asylum recently destroyed by fire. His recommendations included a bill for the establishment of county superintendencies for education, measures to prevent election frauds, and a geological survey of the state. As was the custom, he also reported on the pardons he had granted, a matter he took very seriously.

Hayes was satisfied with the new session of the legislature. He could not prevent its election of Thurman to Wade's place in the Senate, but he managed to induce it to authorize his long-standing request for a geological survey of the state. He continued to seek portraits of former governors and suggested that the legislature authorize a monument to President William H. Harrison at North Bend.

National affairs encouraged him. Wholly satisfied with Grant's inaugural, he thought the cabinet, consisting of three radicals and three conservatives, was organized for work, honesty, and economy. He believed it to be harmonious, and as it did not contain any aspirants for the presidency, he was sure that Grant's leadership was assured. In March, he went to Washington to see matters for himself. Staying for four days, he found the president more completely in accord with Republican ideas than had been expected. Economy and good sense seemed to be in power, he wrote. Then, at the end of May he went to New York. Visiting an art gallery and Stewart's department store, he spent most of two days with the superintendent of police.

Upon his return, he prepared for the upcoming state convention and his renomination. His appointments had already caused him trouble; Colonel Charles Whittlesey, a leading geologist, was so angry at not having been put in charge of the geological survey that he sought to prevent Hayes from becoming governor again. Turning the *Painesville Telegraph* against him, the geologist charged him with free-trade views and maintained that his weakness as a candidate had caused the loss of the state legislature in 1867. Hayes decided that he could disregard the tariff question as a national not a state matter, and in view of Republican losses in other states that year, the other accusation could easily be refuted. It did not seem to hurt him, for on June 23 he was renominated by acclamation. In his address to the convention, he denounced the Democrats' unfulfilled promises, their lengthy legislative sessions, their passage of a visible admixture bill depriving blacks of suffrage, and their taxation policies that burdened the people. Praising the Grant administration, he ran on a platform endorsing the ratification of the Fifteenth Amendment giving the blacks the right to vote. His speech was so well received that he was able to write to his uncle, "Everything connected with the state convention was gratifying enough. It could hardly have been pleasanter."

The subsequent campaign was again a difficult one. After General Rosecrans declined the Democratic nomination, George Hunt Pendleton, the former senator, peace Democrat, and candidate for the vice presidency became Hayes's opponent. His greenback views contrasted sharply with Hayes's hard-money, specie-based outlook. The governor thought Pendleton's nomination would make the race more interesting but also more doubtful. Nevertheless, he maintained his optimism. He delivered speeches in various parts of the state, and though the feminists regarded him as a friend, popular apathy worried him. In the meantime, the legislature had rejected the Fifteenth Amendment, though he hoped its successor would ratify it. In October, he won by a small majority of 7,518 votes and the Republicans recaptured the legislature. Congratulations poured in; his friend William Johnston expected him to run for the Senate within three years.

Because the governors of Ohio did not have an official residence, in November Hayes and his wife moved from 51 East State Street to Judge Noah H. Swayne's house on East Seventh Street, which was a large building with ample grounds. The Hayeses were permitted the use of some of the furniture and did not have to pay an exorbitant rent.

The governor now turned to his inaugural address and began to collect materials on the topics he wished to cover. Then he celebrated Christmas in his new home with all the boys and little Fanny present. It was a most enjoyable occasion.

On January 3, he delivered his message. It followed the outline he had prepared. Recommending taxation and prison reform, he urged the building of more insane asylums, the establishment of an asylum for inebriates and a soldiers' orphans' home. He also advocated the repeal of the visible admixture law, funds for the agricultural and mechanical college, and the ratification of the "just and wise" Fifteenth Amendment. Unlike the previous legislature, the new Republican body enacted many of these suggestions into law. It ratified the amendment on January 27, acted upon a Soldiers' Orphans' Asylum Bill, repealed the visible admixture law, authorized the addition of new wings to the Northern Ohio Lunatic Asylum, and ended the restrictions on voting for soldiers. As Ari Hoogenboom has emphasized, the legislature followed his suggestion to establish the Agricultural and Mechanical College, the predecessor of Ohio State University, of which he considered himself a founder. Hayes had not done badly. In February, he was secure enough to be able to speak from the same platform with Pendleton to the Kentucky state legislature.

The governor was especially interested in the soldiers' and sailors' orphans' homes. Taking great care in the appointment of the board of trustees, he saw to it that Democrats were represented. When his friend General Manning F. Force wrote that he merely supposed Hayes took enough interest in the homes, Lucy protested that "he ought to know that nothing is so near your heart." Hayes was also able to issue warrants for the transfer of juveniles from the penitentiary to a reform school where they were segregated from habitual criminals, a cause in which he had long been interested, commuted several death sentences to lifetime imprisonment, and issued numerous pardons. He was a humane governor. In addition, continuing to further the development of the library, he was a steady proponent of the purchase of the papers of revolutionary general and Northwest Territory governor Arthur St. Clair, which he then transferred to the state library. To enrich the institution, he also started a collection of manuscripts relating to the history of Ohio and its early leading citizens.

As governor, Hayes was naturally involved in various matters of national concern. General John Pope asked him for assistance in defending himself against Fitz-John Porter, who was involved in a long-standing effort to reverse his conviction in 1863 for malfeasance at the second Battle of Bull Run. Wholly convinced of Pope's claims, Hayes answered that Porter's attempts served merely to justify his opponent. He had thought of writing Grant about it, but he really could not add much to the record. Nevertheless, the matter would come to haunt him during his presidential administration. In addition, he advised strongly against forming a new party to deal with the problems of the old. "Whatever shortcomings belong to the record of the Republican party, it is greatly to be preferred at the next election to any party led and ruled, as the Democratic party is, by New York City plunderers," he wrote to his friend Charles Nordhoff. He was certainly not going to support the bolting Liberal Republicans in 1872.

Busy as he was, Hayes managed to find time to engage in genealogical research. He succeeded in tracing his lineage almost to the *Mayflower*, and though he had always thought himself Scottish, he found that on his father's side, thirty of the founding fathers of his family were English, and only two, Hayes and Rutherford, Scottish. In addition, he asked for information of his wife's ancestry, especially the Cooks, her grandfather's forebears.

Late in June, he embarked on another trip to Washington. Visiting General Grant at the White House, he found the president preoccupied with the weather—the heat was unbearable—and the acquisition of Santo Domingo (the Dominican Republic). Realizing that the annexation treaty would not be ratified, Grant expressed his anger at the members of the Senate Foreign Relations Committee. He called Charles Sumner, the chairman, "puffed up and unsound," and labeled Carl Schurz "an infidel and an atheist [who] had been a rebel in his own country—as much a rebel against his government as Jeff Davis." Hayes did not record his reaction, but in view of his later friendship for Schurz, he was apparently unaffected. In fact, together with Schurz he hailed the Prussian victories over the French in the 1870 war. Like most Americans, he had long detested Napoleon III. But he did not lose his respect for Grant. A proud veteran, he could not forget the general's wartime successes.

It was at this time that Hayes for the first time became involved in a labor dispute. When a strike broke out at the Brewster Coal Company in Akron, he telegraphed to authorize the sheriff "to act to preserve the peace." This type of government interference on behalf of employers was then common, and Hayes acted in the manner expected of him, just as he would later proceed as president. But in the long run, he became conscious of the needs of labor and pleaded for justice for the strikers.

Still fond of traveling, Hayes continued with his visits to all manner of sights and locations. He attended military reunions, among them one of the Seventy-ninth regiment of which he had almost become colonel, addressed a *Saengerfest*, a German singing festival, in Cincinnati, and in August undertook a journey to Wisconsin and Minnesota. Accompanied by his close friend General Force, he went to Milwaukee, St. Paul, Superior, and Fond du Lac, and stopped in Duluth, where together with his uncle he had investments in real estate, which, he wrote to Sardis Birchard, had almost doubled in value. In September, he took his son Birch to Cornell, but found that the young man could enter the freshman class only with further studies in Latin and geometry. He promptly hired a tutor, who enabled Birch eventually to do well. In October for several weeks the governor delivered campaign speeches for John Bingham, the moderate Ohio congressman, and in November attended a reunion of the Army of the Cumberland.

Even though the Grant administration was encountering more and more difficulties and became involved in various scandals, Hayes continued to endorse it. With the exception of the president's desire to annex the Dominican Republic, he found Grant's December 1870 message "exceedingly satisfactory to the people" and heard that the administration had built up American prestige in Europe. Even the recall of the historian John Lothrop Motley from the Court of St. James seemed justified. A few months later he praised the administration for "having been faithful on the great question of the rights of the colored people." After all, Grant had upheld congressional Reconstruction.

The governor's 1871 message, delivered on January 3, was similar to his previous ones. Still worried about increases in taxes, he suggested that local authorities, like their state counterparts, ought to be prohibited from creating debts. Praising the progress made in the state's penitentiaries, he again stressed the importance of separating juvenile defenders from hardened criminals. He pleaded once more for funds for the soldiers' orphans' home, lauded the operation of the girls' reform school, and submitted the report of the geological survey of the state. The message was short, and even unfriendly newspapers praised it.

In February, after the birth of still another son, Scott Russell, Hayes went to Washington to arrange for certain appointments, settle some of Ohio's military claims, and look after his uncle Roger Birchard's claims for burned bonds. He saw the president again, found him affable and still hopeful for the annexation of the Dominican Republic. Unfortunately he missed former Secretary of War Edwin M. Stanton, who expressed his regret and his hope to see him next time.

By this time, Hayes had made up his mind to quit politics at the end of his term, as the occasion seemed ripe. Although Charles Nordhoff thought the Republicans were in bad trouble, he disagreed. The main political questions of the time, he replied, were the South, the debt, relations with Great Britain, Santo Domingo, and Grant's appointments. The majority agreed with the administration on the first two of these questions; they regretted the Santo Domingo affair but would accept it, and though they were annoyed about some appointments, they would not desert the party as long as the Republicans were right on the South and the Democrats wrong. Deeming these questions petty in comparison with such former ones as slavery and national supremacy, he was content as long as the country was safe. He thought he could easily be elected to the Senate, but he was unwilling to become a candidate. And even though he was strongly urged to reconsider his declination to run for governor again—"the difficulty in finding a successor for you shows how excellent was our original choice," wrote one of his supporters—he adamantly refused.

As had become his habit, he continued to pursue his interest in his ancestry. He corresponded with cousins and others far and wide to collect a vast amount of knowledge concerning the Hayeses, Birchards, and their relatives. He contemplated a trip to his ancestral sites in Vermont, but unfortunately an eye infection curtailed his activities. He did take another trip to Washington, however, telling all who asked that he was definitely going to retire at the end of his term. The city pleased him, and he predicted that if Washington remained the capital, it would be the finest city in the world in a century or two. In addition, he visited the Shenandoah Valley, to look at the scenes of his wartime experiences and cure his failing health. At the end of June, he attended the commencement at

Kenyon College, and in July finally traveled to Vermont, where he visited his relatives, the cemeteries and houses of his forebears, and then went on to Connecticut for more genealogical researches. From New London he took a steamboat to New York.

In June the Ohio Republican convention nominated Edward Noyes, Hayes's choice, as his successor. Hayes of course took part in the subsequent campaign, delivering speeches blasting the Democrats. At Zanesville in August he said that the so-called New Departure, the alleged acceptance of such Republican principles as the supremacy of the national power, the right of all to vote, and the safeguarding of the public credit, was not the idea of many of the members of the opposition party, and that the people of Ohio were obviously too sophisticated to fall for declarations merely meant to obtain votes. At Cincinnati, participating in the unveiling of the famous Davidson Fountain in the presence of local dignitaries, the archbishop, and a Jewish rabbi, he tried to speak to fifty or sixty thousand people who could hardly hear him. In October Noyes was elected governor, so that Hayes could retire to private life with a clear conscience.

His travels continued. Shortly after the election, he went to Chicago to see the damage inflicted by the great fire and help the sufferers. The conflagration caused great losses to his friend Rogers, with whom he had been building a house in Duluth, and now that Rogers had no money, he had to raise five thousand dollars himself. But as usual, he managed. In November, he went to Lancaster to be a pallbearer at Thomas Ewing's funeral, a task he thought he owed the great statesman who many years earlier, after hearing Hayes's speech in the Summons case, had predicted that he would make his mark in the state.

On the last day of the year 1871, Hayes mused about his career. It was the twentieth year of his married life, and, having held offices for thirteen years, he wanted to leave public life. It had been pleasant, but his expenses had exceeded his income, and he had been unable to devote as much time to his family as he would have liked. But, as

General John Pope wrote to him, popular opinion would never permit him to retire permanently. A great future was still in store for him.

His term was rapidly drawing to a close. On January 1, he sent in his annual message, in which he called for a prohibition of incurring indebtedness by local authorities and asked for the establishment of teachers' schools. Urging penitentiary reform, he also advocated the regulation of railroads and the final completion of buildings for insane asylums and the soldiers' and sailors' orphans' institution. In addition, he suggested the erection of monuments to Ohio Generals Harrison and Thomas L. Hamer, as well as a governor's mansion. A week later he gave a reception for the governor-elect, the legislature, and various notables, and then left office.

His last days had been taken up with the fight for the next senatorship. John Sherman was the leading candidate, but a number of Republicans were anxious to join with some dissatisfied Democrats to elect Hayes. Although admitting to himself that he would like to be a senator, he refused. Nevertheless, in the evening of January 9, after the majority of the Republican caucus had voted for Sherman and after he was already about to retire, the bell rang and two Republicans asked him to reconsider and run. He was sure to be elected, they said, and the next senator would be the next president. Stating that he could not honorably comply, he went to bed, only to be awakened by his uncle's friend John G. Deshler, who once more said a party had been meeting at his house and they would elect him if he consented. Hayes refused again and went to sleep.

In his own mind, he had done a good job as governor. The geological survey, the soldiers' and sailors' orphans' home, the State Board of charities, the agricultural college, and the Fifteenth Amendment were only among a few of the accomplishments of which he was proud. And while his own estimate of his accomplishments was somewhat exaggerated, he had been a competent if not outstanding chief executive.

After leaving Columbus, Hayes moved back to Cincinnati, to the Carlisle House near his old home and established an office at Sixth and Walnut Streets. In March he went to Duluth to look after his investments, took a railroad trip to Dakota Territory in spite of the heavy snow, and visited his friend Rogers. Upon his return, while dabbling in railroad investments, he found time to meet William Cullen Bryant, who discoursed on his poetry and translations. Hayes found him modest, frank, pithy, and friendly and could only admire the poet's looks and manners, to say nothing of his intellect.

But the ex-governor could not stay out of politics. The year 1872 saw the Liberal Republicans' revolt against the Grant administration, provoked by its efforts to annex the Dominican Republic, its failure to carry out civil service reforms, and its dependence on corrupt political machines. The Liberals met in Cincinnati, and Hayes, accompanied by Lucy and other guests, went to watch the proceedings. Nonplussed by the nomination of Horace Greeley for the presidency, he feared that should the editor obtain Democratic support the Liberals might defeat Grant. When the Democrats did indeed endorse the Liberal ticket, his pessimism increased. The upbeat feeling at the Republican national convention in Philadelphia, to which he had been elected a delegate at large, changed his mood, and in August he became a candidate for Congress in the 2nd district. As usual, he tried in vain to decline, but the convention refused to accept his refusal to run and nominated him. Confessing that it was flattering, he accepted the nomination. His friends would have been positively insulted had he refused, he told himself. And though the outlook seemed favorable in the beginning, he gradually began to realize that his chances were not good. He had had to campaign once more in town after town, where he raised the usual issues—black suffrage, a hard currency, civil service reform, and peace in the South. Yet, as he had surmised, in October his opponent, General Henry B. Banning, defeated him. He called his loss his Waterloo, though he ran several hundred votes ahead of the rest of the ticket. It was his first and only electoral defeat.

The next contest was more to his liking. In November, much to Hayes's pleasure, General Grant was reelected. It was also satisfying that he had done better than Grant in his own district. Poor Greeley not only lost his wife but died himself even before the electoral votes could be cast. The Republicans were confident of the future.

Sardis Birchard, Hayes's uncle, was now getting old. His health was deteriorating, and he decided to deed his estate, Spiegel Grove in Fremont, to his nephew. Hayes and his family were to move in the spring of 1873. Hayes immediately decided to enlarge the property, at that time a two-storied building with a gabled roof, a parlor measuring fifteen by twenty feet, and a comfortable living room. He wanted a bigger veranda, parlor, and a library. As his uncle had deeded him some valuable property in Toledo he had no real financial worries, despite frequent indebtedness, and made Fremont his home again in 1873. Suggesting to his uncle that he establish a free library, a project to which he contributed some of his own money, he became an enthusiastic backer of the institution. It was in Fremont that his eighth child, another boy, was born in August. He named him Manning Force, after his longtime friend. Hayes was now engaged in real estate, a profession that satisfied him, although he did not give up all public appearances.

In March of 1873, President Grant appointed Hayes as an assistant treasurer. Although he appreciated the offer, which, he thought, made it possible for him to leave Cincinnati with a well-rounded political record, he declined it. It was too small an office for someone with his previous positions. Naturally, he continued to attend public functions, especially army reunions at which he frequently delivered speeches. Elected president of the Twenty-third Regiment Association, he greatly enjoyed a reunion of the Army of the Tennessee, especially as President Grant asked him to share the reviewing stand with him. But he did not approve of the eulogy of the recently deceased chief justice at the Cincinnati bar's memorial meeting. It was not honest, he said to his friend John W. Herron. While admitting that Chase possessed intellect, culture, and a commanding presence, he nevertheless considered him cold, selfish, and unscrupulous, especially in his relations with Lincoln.

Eighteen seventy-three was a bad year for the country, the state, and the party. When in September the banking house of Jay Cooke collapsed, the nation entered into the most severe depression—panic, as it was then called—in its history. Millions lost their jobs, businesses went into bankruptcy, and the effect on politics was the usual one: the party in power was held responsible. Consequently, that October the Democrats won in Ohio, as they did elsewhere that year, and William Allen, the former senator and peace Democrat was elected governor. Carrying the legislature as well, the Democrats reelected Thurman to the Senate. These developments showed the Republicans that they needed a vote-getter like Hayes if they wanted to succeed again.

Hayes was now very busy in Spiegel Grove. In January his ailing uncle died. He had held his uncle's hand until the last moment, and he was deeply affected by the loss. After settling Sardis Birchard's affairs, he involved himself with the free library, now called the Birchard Library, in the room set aside for it in Birchard Hall. He also cleared some acres behind the house for a fruit garden, pulling up trees and working on the grounds. When it came to politics, he accepted Allen's nomination to serve on the board for the commission of the centennial celebration in Philadelphia in 1876; unlike the Democrats, however, he continued to emphasize his strong stand against any sort of inflation. "I regard the inflation acts as wrong in all ways," he wrote to his uncle Austin in Vermont, even though he himself had many debts and would have benefited by their passage. But, he added, he could stand it if others could. And he rejoiced at Grant's veto of the inflation bill in 1874.

That July, he had the satisfaction of seeing his eldest son Birch graduate from Cornell, where the second, Webb, had already been admitted. But in August his last-born, Manning, died, the third child he lost. In October, he went to New England again, only to return to take part in the campaign of 1874. Speaking in various cities, he hoped to reverse the Democratic trend but was to be disappointed. The canvass ended badly for the Republicans, not only in Ohio but throughout the country, so that the Democrats recaptured the House of Representatives for the first time since before the Civil War. Hayes, who was not directly involved, busied himself with historical research and the education of his children. He took Ruddy, whose weak eyes and delicate health prevented him from going to Harvard or Yale, to Michigan Agricultural College at Lansing, told Webb at Cornell to persevere and study hard, and went sleigh riding with Fanny and Scott in the unusually cold winter.

Of course, he also continued to pursue his private interests. At Lansing, he visited the state prison, satisfying his interests in penology. To his Texan friend Bryan he once again stressed that, as he wrote, "the most important thing in Texas, as everywhere else, is *education for all.*" Yielding to the prejudices of the time, he added, "I, of course, don't believe in forcing whites and blacks together. But both classes should be fully provided for." It was a belief that he attempted to popularize until the end of his life.

His private pursuits were soon to be ended. The Republicans, anxious to regain power, needed a strong and popular candidate, and in March 1875 the Republican caucus at Columbus endorsed him as governor for an unprecedented third term. The distinction attracted him, especially as there was again talk of a possible presidency for the next governor, but as usual he hesitated. "A third term would be a distinction—a feather I would like to wear," he admitted. "No man ever had it in Ohio. Letters tell me I am really wanted. But the present condition of my money matters requires attention. More important still, I do not sympathize with a large share of the party leaders. I hate the corruptionists of whom Butler is the leader. I doubt the ultra measures relating to the South, and I am opposed to the course of General Grant on the third term, the civil service, and the appointment of unfit men or party men on partisan or personal grounds." These considerations reflected the widespread criticism of the scandals that had affected the Grant administration, the salary grab, the Crédit Mobilier, the Whiskey Ring, and other problems. But the Republicans did not let up. They needed an opponent for Governor Allen, and Hayes, with his hard-money ideas, seemed to be the one man to defeat the incumbent. He delivered a Decoration Day address at Toledo, received more requests to run for governor, and on June 2, the state convention nominated him. Considering his chief rival, Judge Alphonso Taft, an able and good man, he protested that he did not want to enter into a contest with the judge, but he was nominated by a vote of 396 to 151, and when he learned that Taft's son had moved this nomination by acclamation, he accepted.

The main issue in the subsequent campaign was the question of finance. The Republican administration of General Grant had clearly indicated its support of sound money and the resumption of specie payments, while the Democrats in Ohio now endorsed greenbacks and the inflation of the currency. Hayes was known for his hard-money views and ably defended them, a task in which he was aided by such outside speakers as Carl Schurz, Senator Morton of Indiana, and John Sherman. He also attacked the Democrats for alleged partiality toward alleged Catholic efforts to supersede the public schools by their support for the totally harmless Geghan Bill allowing the appointment of Catholic priests in schools and penitentiaries. Opening the campaign together with John Sherman at Marion, he delivered a decisive speech advocating these views. "Our motto is, 'Honest money for all, free schools for all,'" he said, while castigating the Democrats for a "violation of all sound financial principles." The campaign then took him to Portsmouth, Beaver, Centerville, Gallipolis, Athens, Cincinnati, Toledo, and other towns. Speaking virtually every day in September, in October he finally prevailed and by a vote of 297,815 to 292,264 was elected governor a third time, carrying both houses of the legislature for the party as well. The victory immediately made him a potential presidential candidate.

Shortly after his election, he went to Pennsylvania to assist the campaign of Governor J. F. Hartranft of Pennsylvania. Enjoying the attention of crowds all over the Keystone State, he contributed to the governor's victory with his speeches. When he came home, Webb joined him after leaving Cornell, and Birch entered law school.

He was inaugurated on January 10. In his inaugural address, he urged a limitation of municipal debts, a decrease in expenditures, and funds for prisons and beneficent institutions. With a friendly legislature, he was able to carry out much of his program. The state debt was reduced, the Geghan Bill was repealed, the Board of Charities reestablished, and he was able to pardon a number of convicts. But even as he felt it was like slipping into old slippers to take his seat in the governor's office once more, at first he was lonely. Lucy, though present for a splendid reception for the legislature by the citizens of Columbus, was still in Fremont and did not come permanently until March. Hayes rented a furnished house at 60 East Broad Street, opposite the State House Square, where he could keep a household with Lucy, Fanny, Scott, and Winnie, the maid. Keeping regular hours once more, he rose between five and seven, wrote letters until breakfast at 8:30, stayed at his office from nine until one, dined at about two, and then stayed in the office again until after five. Evenings were free for calls and callers. In good health, the heavily bearded Hayes weighed about 180 pounds.

In labor relations, despite his considerable sympathy for the less privileged, he was still a child of his age. In April, to control a miners' strike at Massilon, he issued a proclamation announcing that the government would protect laborers in their right to work and property owners in the use and possession of their property and used military force to suppress the disturbance. Otherwise his administration was successful, though after June it was overshadowed by his nomination for the presidency. In his final message, on January 2, 1877, he was able to take credit for the reduction of the state's debt, the establishment of various welfare institutions, and the geological survey. He even took pride in his interference in the coal strike. Suggesting the establishment of intermediate workhouses, he sought to reform the prison system, which he still found inadequate, and advocated a constitutional amendment to change state election days to make them coincide with national ones. All in all, Hayes, now president-elect, still took pride in his governorship.

Hayes had indeed established a creditable though not exceptional record as congressman and governor. Though not yet widely known, he was acknowledged to be honest in a corrupt age and a faithful party member. This reputation would serve him well.

# 4

## The Disputed Election

As one of the four presidential elections in which the electoral vote did not reflect the popular majority or plurality, the election of 1876 is of particular interest. Hayes's involvement in this controversy came about more or less by accident. To be sure, when he first accepted his third nomination for governor of Ohio, his friends assured him that the office might lead to a presidential nomination, but he professed not to be particularly intrigued.

Yet Hayes was not inactive. When Ohio Senator John Sherman, in a letter discussing the presidency, maintained that his military record was not distinguished, he immediately prepared a summary of his service and accomplishments during the war for the use of his supporters. Stressing his command of a regiment that successfully opened the Battle of South Mountain, as well as that of a brigade at Cloyd's Mountain, he highlighted his covering of the retreat of Crook's army after the defeat at Winchester. To set the record straight, he also expressed pride in his command of one of the two brigades selected by Sheridan to lead in attacks on Early in the Shenandoah Valley and his feats at Berryville and Winchester, Fisher's Hill and Cedar Creek. He rapidly won Sherman over. And although it appeared that the leading candidates, James G. Blaine, Oliver Morton, and Roscoe Conkling, made any Hayes candidacy most doubtful, as Ben Butler, the controversial Massachusetts politician, wrote to his son-in-law, Governor Adelbert Ames of Mississippi, a large number of Ohio county conventions elected delegates to the state convention who expressed their preference for the governor. Hayes did not expect to go beyond this complimentary stage, but he did think that the vice presidency was a possibility. "The vice presidency seems to be conceded to me on all sides, or nearly so . . . ," he mused. "However, the thoughts of my friends are on the first place." Many hard-money advocates, among them James A. Garfield, the later president, as well as John Sherman, favored his candidacy; the state convention, at which his son Webb was present, endorsed him in March; and he was the second choice of many others. "We are in danger of losing our heads, I suppose," he wrote, "but I do not feel any dangerous symptoms. Indeed I would now like to be well out of it."

His prevarication was his usual response to any candidacy. When he wrote that he was not "in that 'local' folly known as the Hayes movement," he was not being quite ingenuous. The national convention was to be held in Cincinnati, which had long been his hometown and would thus place him at an advantage, and he was constantly being told that his chances were improving. To make sure that he would be well represented there, he asked Sherman to attend. Though he wrote that he merely wanted him to be present to be able to withdraw his candidacy when the time came and informed supporters that he was going to remain entirely passive during the campaign, it was one way of furthering his cause. And he mended his fences with possible competitors, writing a note of sympathy to Blaine, the main contestant, who had suffered a heat stroke on the way from church. His eyes were almost blinded with tears about the mishap, he asserted.

The Republican national convention met on June 14. Hayes had told his supporters he did not want second place, and though still maintaining that he was perfectly indifferent to the result, he had a well-organized group of friends at the meeting, headed by former Governor Edward F. Noyes, who made the nominating speech for him. Presenting him as a brave veteran, Noyes stressed his repeated defeats of Democratic contenders for governor. "He is a gentleman who has fallen into the habit of defeating Democratic aspirants for the presidency; and we in Ohio all have a notion, that, from long experience, he will be able to do it again," said the Ohioan, and his points were repeated by Benjamin F. Wade, who seconded the nomination. At first, it did not seem likely that Hayes would win; the seeming favorite was Blaine. Nominated by Robert G. Ingersoll as the "plumed knight" from the state of Maine, the Maine congressman was a distinguished candidate. He had been in Congress since 1863, had served as Speaker of the House, and was an excellent and popular speaker. But he had a dubious past because of his involvement in favors to various railroads. Governor Morton of Indiana was another hopeful. A founder of the Republican party, he had kept the Copperheads in check during the Civil War, and, though paralyzed by a stroke, had been a radical senator during the entire Reconstruction period. Grant's former secretary of the interior, Benjamin H. Bristow of Kentucky, was still another contender, favored by the reform element because of his breakup of the Whiskey Ring during his tenure at the Interior Department. The eloquent leader of the New York Republican machine, Roscoe Conkling, who had long been one of Grant's favorites, was also in the running, as was Governor John F. Hartranft of Pennsylvania, a favorite son, and Postmaster General Marshall Jewell, the able former governor of Connecticut, who withdrew after the first ballot.

The rivalry between these candidates worked to Hayes's advantage. On the first ballot Blaine obtained 285 votes to Hayes's 61, Morton's 125, Bristow's 113, Conkling's 99, Hartranft's 58, and Jewell's 11. On the second, Blaine's vote increased to 296, Hayes gained two votes, while that of the others did not change much. The voting continued in pretty much the same fashion until the fifth ballot, when Hayes garnered 104 to Blaine's 286. Blaine rallied to receive 308 on the next round, but fell short of the 379 necessary for a choice. He could have been nominated that evening; however, led by Don Cameron of Pennsylvania, his opponents succeeded in calling for an adjournment. On the next day, on the seventh ballot, Blaine's antagonists converged on Hayes and gave him 384 votes, thus clinching his nomination. William Wheeler of New York, a longtime member of the state legislature and of Congress, was selected for second place, though Hayes hardly knew him. When in January he had first heard of the possibility of a Hayes-Wheeler ticket, his comment had been, "I am ashamed to say, who is *Wheeler?*" He would soon become friendly with his running mate.

The platform upon which the candidates were to run mirrored Hayes's long-held opinions. Reaffirming that the United States was a nation, not a league, it endorsed equal rights for all, the pacification of the South, and pledged the resumption of specie payments and the earliest redemption of United States notes in coin. It strongly endorsed the separation of powers in making appointments, the president to make nominations and the Senate to advise and consent, called for equal rights for women, and advocated the prohibition of the use of public funds for sectarian schools. In addition, it praised the Grant administration and accused the Democrats of having sympathized with the Southern rebellion.

Back in Columbus, Hayes was awaiting results. The first ballot seemed to indicate Blaine's success. "This relieves me perceptively," he wrote. But realizing very soon that his nomination was more than a possibility, he became cheerful and slept well. Then, alone in the governor's office, receiving more and more encouraging dispatches from various friends, he became more absorbed, and did not sleep again. When he was nominated, on Friday, June 17, he mused that Friday was his lucky day and was deeply touched by Blaine's congratulations. "Poor Blaine," he wrote to his son Birch, while his hand was sore from shaking hands of well-wishers. Enthusiastic crowds serenaded him and letters of congratulation poured in from all directions.

The Republican press generally accepted the nomination with satisfaction. "History repeats itself after all," wrote the *New York*

*Times.* "In 1876 as in 1860 the Republican party has found its Lincoln to lead it on to victory." Calling Hayes a man of plain, unobtrusive manners, unimpeachable honesty, keen intelligence, and robust common sense, the *Times* praised his military background and lauded his administrative record. The *Cincinnati Gazette* expressed its satisfaction with the nomination of a candidate of high character worthy of the confidence of the country, and the *Cincinnati Commercial* congratulated the Republicans upon their choice. "They have not made the strongest nomination possible," it said, "but perhaps the best of which the party is capable." The *New York Evening Post* agreed. Asserting that the Republicans had narrowly escaped a fatal error, as Blaine could not have been elected, it labeled Hayes a fit man and an available candidate.

When John Sherman wrote his memoirs in the 1890s, he still believed "that the nomination of Hayes was not only the safest, but the strongest that could be made. . . . Hayes had growing qualities, and in every respect was worthy of the high position of President. . . . Among all the public men with whom I have been before in contact, I have known none who was freer from personal objection, whose character was more stainless, who was better adapted for a high executive office, than Rutherford B. Hayes."

The opposition, particularly the *New York Sun*, thought the nominee's weakness and unimportance were his principal recommendations. It did, however, admit that Hayes was honest and well liked. "It is a strong ticket," the *Sun* conceded, predicting that the candidate would get the vote of every Republican and of many independents. Democratic papers, as was to be expected, referred to him as a "dishwater candidate" and accused him of religious bigotry.

Shortly after his nomination, Hayes went to Fremont, where another enthusiastic welcome awaited him. In a speech to his neighbors, he thanked them for their reception, reminded them of his coming to town with Sardis Birchard, and assured them that if elected, he would be looking forward to returning to Spiegel Grove.

On June 28, at St. Louis, the Democrats nominated Governor Samuel J. Tilden of New York to contest the presidency with Hayes. A bachelor who had long been active in the Democratic party, Tilden had gained his reputation as a reformer by first breaking up the Tweed Ring and then the state's equally corrupt Canal Ring. Described by John Sherman as a man of singular political sagacity and great shrewdness, he was also recognized as a capable money-maker. The *New York Herald* called him "one of the ablest and most astute managers that have ever appeared in the politics of this country," while the reform record of both candidates pleased the *New York Evening Post*, which commented that better elements had prevailed in St. Louis as well as in Cincinnati. "The decencies of the canvass are thus guaranteed," it said. Hayes was less enthusiastic. He realized that the nomination of Tilden meant "a hot and critical contest," which made the states of New York, Connecticut, and New Jersey doubtful. He decided immediately to compose his letter of acceptance so that it would appear prior to Tilden's.

The letter, for which he had sought advice from Carl Schurz and George William Curtis, both reformers who highlighted the importance of civil service reform, fully expressed his ideas and became his standard reply to all questions during the campaign. Stressing his great interest in civil service reform, he pledged that if elected he would use all the powers of the executive in its favor. Regarding the financial question, he asserted that he regarded "all the laws of the United States relating to the payment of the public indebtedness, the legal tender notes included, as constituting a pledge and moral obligation of the Government, which must in good faith be kept," and strongly endorsed the resumption of specie payments. Then he turned to the Southern question. Endorsing the convention's resolution of the permanent pacification of the country and the complete protection of all its citizens in the free enjoyment of all their constitutional rights, he pledged, "Let me assure my countrymen in the Southern States that if I shall be charged with the duty of organizing an administration, it will be one which will regard and cherish their truest interests—the interests of the white and colored people both, and equally; and which will put forth its best efforts in behalf of a civil policy which will wipe out forever the distinction between North and South in our common country." In addition, he favored an amendment placing the schools beyond the danger of sectarian control and promised not to seek a second term.

Although the letter was generally well received, General Sickles criticized it for its failure to arouse Republican Civil War enthusiasm, and the reference to a one-term limit miffed General Grant, then serving for the second time. Hayes tried to assuage him by explaining he was merely attempting to please his competitors for the nomination, generally younger than he, by giving them a chance to compete in 1880, and Grant seemed satisfied.

Hayes was not too sanguine about the contest. The financial panic boded ill for the party in power; corruption in Washington, especially the impeachment of Secretary of War William W. Belknap, who had sold Indian offices, was held against the Republicans, and the greenback issue threatened to diminish votes in Indiana and Ohio. Schurz urged greater emphasis on civil service reform and complained about assessments of public employees, a practice Hayes condemned, though he was unable to stop it. He himself thought the controlling sentiment was the apprehension that a Democratic victory would bring the rebellion into power, and he wanted the campaign conducted with this popular fear in mind, although he remained passive, as was the custom for presidential hopefuls.

His supporters waged a strong campaign. His cousin by marriage, William Dean Howells, wrote a campaign biography, as did J. Q. Howard and Russell H. Conwell. William Henry Smith, now in charge of the Western Associated Press in Chicago, worked hard for his old friend, and Carl Schurz and others, including some of the rivals for his nomination, continued to deliver speeches in his behalf.

It was unavoidable that Hayes had to defend himself against any number of spurious charges. Because of his stand against sectarian influence in the schools, he was suspected of nativism. His secretary had to deny categorically that Hayes ever was a Know-Nothing, or that he had given assurances of sympathy with declarations against the naturalization of foreigners and the privileges of naturalized citizens. Again accused of xenophobia for allegedly having joined the nativist American Alliance, he refuted imputations of xenophobia once more, although his secretary had indeed written a letter acknowledging the organization's endorsement. Hayes of course had never joined the Alliance, and while he disclaimed all religious prejudice, he insisted on keeping the schools free from sectarian influence. Yet he had to assert again and again that he was free from prejudice and merely opposed sectarian influence in the schools. The matter was especially vital because of the importance of the German vote, part of which was Republican, and the candidate drafted a statement of his tolerant ideas for the St. Louis *Westliche Post*, Schurz's newspaper. A more troublesome accusation was the charge that Hayes had kept the money and two watches confiscated from a deserter executed during the war. The *Chicago Times* published his 1869 correspondence concerning the canard, which he had refuted as a blackmail attempt; now that it had been renewed while he was running for the presidency, he gave an interview to a reporter of the *Cincinnati Commercial* to explain the details of the situation, as far as he could remember them. The four hundred dollars taken from a deserter who was executed at Monocacy Junction, Maryland, in August 1864, if his recollections were correct, had been used to find another recruit, and the watches must still be in the hands of Mr. W. W. Harper of Hartford City, West Virginia, who vainly had been trying to find the deserter's mother. Questions were also raised about his property tax returns for1874–1876; he had to make a thorough investigation of his records and sent his friend Buckland a full account of his returns for various years.

An added difficulty was the situation in New York. Considered crucial in any election because of its large electoral vote, the Empire State was in doubt because of the passive behavior of Roscoe Conkling, the most powerful of its political leaders. Maintaining he was ill, and irked because of his failure to receive the nomination, Conkling took little part in the campaign. On August 13, Hayes wrote him that he was needed both in Ohio and Indiana, but Conkling did little to help. It was a serious loss.

Indiana was an equally difficult problem. Senator Morton told Hayes that the situation there was most grave; that the Greenback party was drawing four-fifths of its votes from the Republicans, and that if they failed in Indiana in October, they would lose the presidency in November. Asked for the remedy, he replied money was needed to employ speakers, a sum of some one hundred thousand dollars, which Hayes considered impossible to raise. But he thought that even if Indiana were lost, he would still have a chance if he carried New York and warned William H. Smith not to emphasize the importance of the October states, of which Indiana was one.

In spite of many signs of a possible defeat, Hayes kept his spirits up. Though fully aware of the possibility of losing—he maintained that he was almost hoping for it because independence as a private citizen was something to look forward to—he was greatly encouraged in September by a Republican success in Maine. "How gloriously you have done!" he wrote to Blaine, adding that general dread of the South gave him hope of victory. Murat Halstead's emphasis on the Southern question in the *Cincinnati Commercial* and Whitelaw Reid's help in the *New York Tribune* also cheered him. Then Howells's book came out, and its subject was very pleased with it. On September 24, anxiously contemplating the end of the contest, he deemed the general drift of events favorable. Prepared for either outcome, he continued his activities as governor of Ohio, the extradition of felons, the visits to new charitable institutions, and remained in his office at Columbus. "I am less and less solicitous on personal grounds about the results," he wrote to Bryan, to whom he asserted that if the South observed the Civil War and Reconstruction amendments, there would be no trouble between the sections. At home, always lonely when Lucy was not with him, he had Webb's help. He enjoyed little Scott's skills with his new three-wheeled velocipede, wrote encouraging letters to Ruddy who had finally gone to Cornell, and supervised Fanny's progress at school.

The October elections were somewhat inconclusive. Contrary to expectations, in Indiana the Republicans carried the legislature and the majority of the congressional delegation, although the Democrats won the state vote as a whole, and Ohio went Republican. Greatly encouraged, Hayes hoped Murat Halstead would speak in New York, a state that still seemed to be the key to final success.

In view of what was to happen later, on October 22 he had a strange premonition. "Another danger is imminent," he wrote. "A contested result. And we have no such means for its decision as ought to be provided by law." Just two Sundays prior to the election, he still found himself cool and indifferent about it, though he thought a Democratic success would be a calamity. Accompanied by Lucy, Webb, Fanny, Scott, and his African-American servants, he calmly went to the Ohio Day celebration at the Philadelphia Centennial, where he made half a dozen speeches from the steps of the Ohio building, but came back feeling that he would probably lose. Fraud in the North and violence in the South would do him in, he thought. For once, he was not as optimistic as usual, although he received constant letters informing him of the imminent success of the campaign.

Then came Election Day, November 7. "Dies irae," he entered in his diary, day of wrath. And that it was. When the first returns came in, he was sure that he had been defeated. Although the Republicans had clearly carried many important Northern states, including Ohio, they had lost New York, Indiana, Connecticut, and New Jersey, and apparently the South as well. He went to bed at twelve to console Lucy, who, as he did, felt great anxiety about the blacks in the South, and the next morning went to his office as usual. "You will wish to know how we feel since the defeat," he wrote to Ruddy at Cornell. "Scott Russell is rejoiced because now we can remain in Columbus where the cousins and friends live. . . . Fanny shares this feeling, but has a suspicion that something desirable has been lost. Birch and Webb don't altogether like it, but are cheerful and philosophical about it. Your mother and I have not been disappointed in the result, however much we would have preferred it to have been otherwise. . . . We escape a heavy responsibility, severe labors, great anxiety and care, and a world of obliging by defeat. We are now free and independent and at peace with all the world, and the rest of mankind."

But his pessimism, if such it was, was premature. As has often been reported, most recently by Ari Hoogenboom and Jerome Sternstein, General Daniel Sickles, returning from the theater after supper to the Fifth Avenue Hotel, Republican headquarters in New York, read the dispatches and found that the Republicans could still win if they could hold some Southern states and those in the far West where the returns had not yet come in. Attaching Zachariah Chandler's signature, he telegraphed to Republican leaders in South Carolina, Florida, Louisiana, and Oregon that Hayes was elected if their states could be held and asked them to do so. The next morning, this procedure was repeated by John C. Reid of the *New York Times*, who had also doubted reports of defeat and came to Republican headquarters to find William E. Chandler, just arrived from New Hampshire. Together they woke Zach Chandler and also sent telegrams to Florida, Louisiana, South Carolina, Oregon, and Nevada to hold these states.

"Results still uncertain," wrote the *New York Times* that morning, stating that it had reason to claim 181 electoral votes for the Republicans and to concede 184 to the Democrats, but that Florida was still undecided. On November 9 its headline read, "THE BATTLE

WON," claiming victory in Florida. Other papers were less certain, the *New York Herald* headlining, "THE RESULT: WHAT IS IT?" and the Democratic *Sun* picturing Tilden as president-elect.

And Hayes? Having arrived at his office content with his belief in failure, as time went on, he heard that all was not lost. At 6:10 P.M. he received a telegram from William E. Chandler that the Republicans had won in Florida and South Carolina as well as in Oregon and Louisiana so that they had the 185 votes necessary for election. At 8:00 P.M., Sickles also sent a confirmatory telegram, and soon Hayes received congratulations from various friends. A crowd gathered outside to cheer and Hayes addressed them by saying nothing was certain yet, but that if defeated he would live happily among his evident friends for the next year and a half.

The controversy was not settled in the days to come. The main problem was the result in the three Southern states that had not yet been "redeemed" by the Democrats, South Carolina, Louisiana, and Florida. In each one of these, there were returning boards, political bodies authorized to throw out dubious votes and those obtained by violence. If all three were to be retained by the Republicans, Hayes and Wheeler would have 185 electoral votes to Tilden's 184, and thus win the election in spite of Tilden's popular majority of 4,300,590 to 4,036,298. Hayes's supporters were confident; as William H. Bigelow wrote him on November 10, it seemed perfectly clear that he would be the next president. Two days later, Dennison added, "You are undoubtedly elected next President of the United States. Desperate efforts are being made to defeat you in Louisiana, South Carolina, and Florida, but they will not succeed." Samuel Shellabarger agreed, adding that only revolution and war could prevent a Hayes victory.

In view of the importance of the disputed states, both parties sent representatives to the South to supervise the counting of the votes. President Grant himself asked a number of Republican "visiting statesmen" to go to New Orleans, among them James A. Garfield and John Sherman. They traveled immediately to the

Crescent City, where they were joined by other members of the party, including Stanley Matthews, Lew Wallace, and Edward Noyes, as well as an equal number of Democrats sent by Chairman Abram S. Hewitt. They attended each session of the returning board and convinced themselves that that body was acting fairly. In a number of parishes, it was evident that violence and intimidation had kept many blacks from voting, and accordingly the board threw out these returns. A Democratic majority of more than six thousand was thereby converted to a Republican one. William E. Chandler went to Florida and others to South Carolina. Hayes was convinced that in a fair election he would have won the popular as well as the electoral vote, which he thought would have reached two hundred, but that the Democrats had so intimidated the blacks that they rolled up majorities in states that should have been Republican. Though not yet sure of the result, on November 13, thanking W. H. Smith for invaluable help, he added, "I think a fair canvass of the result will still give us the 185 votes required to elect." Anxious to avoid fraud, he strongly expressed his opposition to any movement to influence the returning board. He told Garfield on his way to Louisiana that he did not want any undue influence, and said to John Sherman, also on his way to Louisiana, that if Tilden was elected he desired him by all means to have the office. "Let Mr. Tilden have the place by violence, intimidation, and fraud, rather than prevent it by means that will not bear the purest scrutiny," he insisted. Then he asked Carl Schurz, whom no one could accuse of corruption, to go to New Orleans, but the German American was unable to comply. Having recently lost his wife, he had to take care of his children. On their way back from New Orleans, several of the visiting statesmen, including Sherman and Garfield, came to see Hayes in Columbus. Assuring him of the fairness of the board's conduct, they reemphasized their conviction that he was lawfully entitled to the electoral vote of Louisiana, in spite of the apparent popular Democratic majority in that state. Hayes was easily convinced, but he was not optimistic: "While I have no doubt we are entitled to the victory my impression is that the chances are against us," he confided to Birch. He thought bribery would deprive him of victory.

On December 6, the electors submitted their votes, including those of the three disputed states, in which the returning boards claimed all three for Hayes. But the Democrats also sent in their electoral votes, and Congress was faced with the task of deciding which of the two to count. This created great difficulties. The Democrats were unwilling to yield and insisted that their returns were the proper ones. In addition, there were two governments in both Louisiana and South Carolina, the Republican one, headed by Stephen B. Packard in Louisiana and Daniel Chamberlain in South Carolina, backed by the federal government and challenged by the Democrats backing Francis T. Nicholls in Louisiana and Wade Hampton in South Carolina. The legality of these claims as well as those of the rival returns would have to be determined. An additional problem developed in Oregon, where one of the Republican electors was found to have been a postmaster, and thus ineligible for service. The Democratic governor then appointed a Democrat to join the Republican electors, so that the state's vote would consist of two for Hayes and one for Tilden, thus electing the latter. The Republican electors, however, refused to abide by this action and promptly reelected their rejected colleague who had resigned his postmastership.

Just who was to decide the dispute was unclear. The Constitution was of little help; it merely mandated that the electoral votes were to be transmitted to the president of the Senate, who was to open all the certificates in the presence of both houses, and that the votes should then be counted. At the close of the Civil War, Congress had adopted the so-called twenty-second rule, providing that a majority in either house could refuse to count in a state without debate, but the Senate reversed that rule in 1875, substituting a provision that only a vote of the two houses could reject a state's vote. As the Senate was Republican, the Republicans asserted that its presiding officer, Senator Thomas W. Ferry of Michigan, should count the votes, but the Democratic House contradicted this method, and a deadlock resulted.

Throughout the controversy, Hayes continued to believe firmly that he had been honestly elected, though he doubted the Democrats would yield. Repeatedly affirming the justice of his claim, he was entirely satisfied with the returning boards' reports and disregarded warnings that there were assassination plots against him. Garfield reassured him. He wrote that he could imagine how heavily the great burden of anxiety must rest on Hayes's mind, but he had the utmost confidence and believed in ultimate success. In Florida, the case was clear beyond question; Oregon could be taken care of, and Conkling's sulking and his influence upon Grant was also manageable. Refusing to go to Washington in spite of the advice of some of his friends, Hayes determined to stay quietly in Ohio and not issue any statements about his policies or probable cabinet until the result was announced in February. His letter of acceptance, he insisted, clearly indicated his stand on the South.

In view of the fact that the uncertainty was creating great unease in the country and that there was already talk of a possible armed conflict, Congress was anxious to find a way out, and both houses appointed committees to work out a procedure to solve the problem. The two committees met in January, and on the eighteenth, the joint committee submitted its report to the Senate. It provided for an electoral commission to decide all disputed counts, with only the vote of the two houses able to overrule it. The commission was to consist of seven Republicans and seven Democrats, and with hope one independent. It was to be staffed by three Republican and two Democratic senators, three Democratic and two Republican members of the House, two Supreme Court justices of both parties, and one independent justice, expected to be David Davis of Illinois. Davis, however, was elected a Democratic senator from Illinois at the last moment, so that the third justice was the Republican

Joseph P. Bradley of New Jersey. Thus there were seven Democrats and eight Republicans on the commission.

Most Republicans were initially opposed to this solution. Hayes thought it was unconstitutional. "The compromise report by the Joint Committee, seems to be a surrender, at least, in part, of the case," he argued. "The leading constitutional objection to it, perhaps, is that the appointment of the Commission by act of Congress violates that part of the Constitution which gives the appointment of all other officers to the President." Moreover, he had had no confidence in the committee of Congress setting it up, especially as Roscoe Conkling, who was known to be hostile to him, was a member of it. That Conkling's brilliant speech in its favor contributed to its establishment did not help. Moreover, there was always the chance that the Democrats would refuse to accept any decision contrary to their conviction that they had won—they claimed the majority of the popular vote—and they could always filibuster to delay the inauguration of a new president.

As C. Vann Woodward has shown, even before the commission reported, various Hayes friends had already been negotiating with Southern representatives, men like Colonel A. J. Kellar of the *Memphis Avalanche* and Arthur S. Colyar, a prominent Memphis lawyer, who were willing to permit a Republican presidency provided they received certain assurances of economic and other aid. They were especially interested in subsidies for the construction of the Texas Pacific Railroad. Hayes himself heard that several old Southern Whigs were ready to support him. Although he refused to commit himself beyond his statements in his letter of acceptance, he did tell his friend and chief manager Smith, who was involved in these negotiations, that he would be exceptionally liberal about education and internal improvements of a national character.

The principal question before the commission, which patiently listened to able speeches of advocates of both sides, Stanley Matthews being especially effective, was whether it was willing to go behind the reported votes. The matter became crucial when the commission reached the vote of Florida. Justice Bradley held the casting vote; after reflecting during the night, on February 7 he announced that he was unwilling to examine the background of the state's returns but would accept them as reported. Whether the Republicans put undue pressure on him has been debated ever since. At any rate, his decision in this case, as well as in that of the other disputed states of South Carolina, Louisiana, and Oregon, went far toward securing Hayes's election.

As there was still a danger of a Democratic filibuster, a final meeting between certain Southerners, among them Henry Watterson, Benjamin Harvey Hill, John B. Gordon, Lucius Q. C. Lamar, and representatives of the would-be president—Garfield, Matthews, John Sherman, and Charles Foster—met at Wormley's Hotel on February 26 to confirm various agreements made earlier. Matthews assured the Southerners that as a close friend of Hayes he knew what the governor was going to do. He would recognize Governor Nicholls and federal troops would be withdrawn. In return the Southerners promised to respect freedmen's rights and elect a Republican Senator. Although C. Vann Woodward, in his book *Reunion and Reaction,* has proven that this conference was not as important as had formerly been assumed, the meeting restated previous important agreements; and most certainly Hayes, although his supporters did express his ideas, was not directly implicated in it.

It was not till 4:10 in the morning of March 2 that the vote count was finally completed, the Democrats having held up the decision on Vermont and Wisconsin by challenging the eligibility of two Hayes electors. Senator Ferry, the president pro tem of the Senate, announced the result of 185 votes for Hayes and 184 for Tilden. Then the weary members of Congress went home. "The country feels more restful today than it has felt for months," exulted the *New York Evening Post.* "President Hayes is about to take possession of his office. Let it be understood once and for all that he takes it without a cloud on his title." Other Republican papers agreed—the Democrats had lost standing with their disgusting game, was the opinion of the *New York Tribune*, which was certain that Hayes had gained in public opinion and could be trusted. The opposition, however, presented an entirely different point of view. "THE FRAUD CONSUMMATED," headlined the *New York Sun* on March 2, three days later adding, "MR. HAYES IS NOT PRESIDENT." It would never give up its campaign against the "great fraud." The *New York World* was also totally critical: "The Electoral Commission has completed its work," it asserted, "and we do not believe there is one candid and competent person outside of the heated circle of partisans who will hesitate, after careful examination of its final judgments submitted to Congress, to say that its official record disgraces every member of the majority of the body."

Hayes, who had rendered his annual message as usual on January 2, finally resigned from the governorship on March 1. That day, accompanied by some of his closest friends, he left for Washington in two special cars attached to a passenger train. Not having heard the final result of the vote count, he told the assembled well-wishers at the Columbus station that he might be back soon and pleaded for a union of hearts. Large crowds cheered him at various towns on the way to the capital, where he arrived on a rainy day a little after nine in the morning on March 2. Welcomed by Dennison, General and Senator Sherman, he went to the senator's house and had breakfast. Afterward, he visited the president and went to the Capitol. He was to be inaugurated on March 5, the fourth being a Sunday, but he took his oath on the previous Saturday. No matter how much the Democrats in and out of Congress might accuse him of fraud, he never had any doubt about the legitimacy of his election.

The final verdict on the dispute has never been unanimous. Such writers as Hamilton J. Eckenrode, A. M. Gibson, and Lloyd Robinson have always condemned the Republicans on the grounds that the popular verdict was clearly in favor of Tilden and that the New Yorker should have obtained the electoral votes of the Southern states as well; but as early as 1906 Paul L. Haworth came to the conclusion that the exclusion of the black vote in various Southern states rendered Hayes's victory legitimate. Barnard based his defense of his hero on the constitutionality of the commission, and Ari Hoogenboom, like Haworth, determined that Hayes would probably have won in a fair election. It seems evident that the violence against the blacks and their intimidation not only produced popular majorities in Louisiana, Florida, and South Carolina, but in other states, particularly Mississippi, as well. Thus Hayes entered on his office rightfully—his confidence in his victory was eminently justified.

What strikes a modern observer is the similarity between the election of 1876 and that of 2000. In both cases, the candidate with the seeming popular majority lost; the problem of racial discrimination at the polls influenced both elections, and the state of Florida played a crucial role. Accusations of the opposition's abandonment of its insistence on states' rights, the Democrats in 1877 and the Republicans in 2000, were also parallel. Moreover, both defeated candidates immediately left the field, Tilden by traveling to Europe and Al Gore by disappearing from the news for several months. And in both cases the Supreme Court was involved, with charges of the violation of states' rights. What was different was the aftermath. In 1876, the defeated Democrats did not want to give up the struggle for the presidency and sought to oust Hayes; in 2001, the Democrats not only acquiesced but eventually rallied to the president. But the problem of who was to decide the count has never been satisfactorily solved.

# 5

---

# The Presidency:
# First Two Years

Monday, March 5, 1877, was a cold day in Washington, with thick clouds overhead, and an occasional fine flake of snow in the air, but fortunately no wind. A great crowd had assembled to witness the inauguration of the nineteenth president of the United States, whose disputed title had caused him to receive death threats. Disregarding these, Hayes calmly delivered his inaugural address. It was a speech that in many ways restated the main points of his letter of acceptance. Stressing the primary importance of the pacification of the country and the solution of the problems of the South, he insisted that the constitutional rights of citizens of both races be respected. As he put it, "The permanent pacification of the country upon such principles and by such measures as will secure the complete protection of all its citizens in the free enjoyment of all their constitutional rights is now the one subject in our public affairs which all thoughtful and patriotic citizens regard as of supreme importance."

Universal suffrage required universal education, he insisted, pleading for free schools supported by state governments and, if necessary, supplemented by federal aid. Civil service reform, a major item in his thinking, came next. Although the president owed his election to a party, he sought a degree of nonpartisanship by coining the phrase, "He serves his party best who serves his country best." He strongly endorsed the resumption of specie payments, advocated an amendment for a six-year term for the presidency, and endorsed President Grant's negotiations with foreign nations to settle international disputes. Finally, he recurred to the disputed election and expressed his gratification that the controversy had been settled by a legal process. He spoke clearly and forcibly, and then went to the White House for lunch with the Grants.

The inaugural speech was well received. Congratulatory letters arrived from various parts of the country, and the Republican press joined in the praise. "There have been few inaugural addresses superior to that of President Hayes in mingled wisdom, force, and moderation in statement," wrote *Harper's Weekly*, echoing others who agreed. "The address with which President Hayes begins his official career as Chief Executive of the United States will strengthen the favorable impressions made by his selections for his Cabinet, and give a fresh impulse to the revival of hope and cheerfulness throughout the country," commented the *New York Tribune*. And although the *Tribune* expressed the opinion that even Democrats liked it, opposition newspapers continued their attacks and dwelled on what they called the abandonment of the Negroes. The *New York Sun* regretted that he was a "fraud," otherwise the Democrats and independents might rescue him.

The new president made a good appearance. "President Hayes is a man of medium height, a little stouter than we supposed, with slightly florid complexion, and healthful, manly, and unassuming," wrote the *Pittsburgh Methodist Recorder* shortly after his assumption of office. "He is a gentleman of evident culture. . . . His eye has tenderness and depth of expression which arrests and holds attention. . . . His voice is deep and rich." The Washington correspondent Benjamin Perley Poore added that he was well built, "of stalwart form, open countenance ruddy with health, kind blue eyes, a full, sandy beard in which there were a few silver threads, a well-shaped mouth, and a smile on his lips."

When he first moved into the White House, the mansion's employees were greatly relieved. They saw that there would be a recognition of meritorious service and no dismissals. While his young son Scott might be full of mischief, the new president was obviously a reasonable man who kept his promises.

The first difficulty the new chief executive encountered concerned his choice of a cabinet. Determined not to include any members of the old administration or presidential candidates, nor make an appointment "to take care" of anybody, he disregarded all forms of special pleading and selected various advisers whose alleged independence had impressed him. William M. Evarts, the eminent New York lawyer who had defended Andrew Johnson and then served as his attorney general, became secretary of state; John Sherman, his longtime supporter, secretary of the Treasury; George W. McCrary, an Iowa congressman who had taken a prominent part in the establishment of the electoral commission, secretary of war; and, to please Senator Morton, whose withdrawal had led to Hayes's nomination, Richard W. Thompson, an Indiana ex-Whig and Republican, secretary of the navy. For secretary of the interior, he chose Carl Schurz, the famous German-American senator and Liberal Republican; and for attorney general, Charles Devens, a Massachusetts judge and severely wounded former general. In order to show his goodwill toward the South, at first he wanted to elevate General Joseph E. Johnston to some post, but the opposition was too strong, and he appointed David M. Key, a Tennessee ex-Confederate as postmaster general instead.

These selections, and especially Schurz, Evarts, and Key, caused a row in Congress. Many Stalwarts and traditional Republicans, particularly Conkling, Cameron, Blaine, and Logan, considered Schurz's activities as a Liberal Republican unforgivable, and they had similar feelings about Evarts, who was a prime opponent of Roscoe Conkling and his machine in New York. Hayes thus managed to alienate both factions of the Republican party, the Stalwarts, followers of Roscoe Conkling, the powerful party boss of New York, and the

Half-Breeds, led by James G. Blaine, the senator from Maine. The two leaders had long been enemies; "Lord Roscoe," as his biographer, David M. Jordan, called him, characterizing him as sarcastic, tall, handsome, "haughty, larger than life," and an excellent speaker, had been grossly insulted by Blaine, who referred to his "majestic, supereminent, overpowering turkey-like strut," a slur the New Yorker had never forgiven. But both Blaine and Conkling had been disappointed by not having been nominated to the presidency. According to David Saville Muzzey, Blaine ranked "with the very greatest Speakers of the House. . . . His courtesy was unfailing, his temper unruffled, and his command of parliamentary law and procedure unimpeachable." But he had long been suspected of corruption in connection with certain railroad bonds, and though nothing was ever proved against him, the rumor probably kept him from the presidency. Hayes might have assuaged both by appointing either of them to the cabinet, but he was determined to show his independence, thus complicating his relations with Congress at the very beginning. This became evident when, contrary to usual custom, the cabinet nominations were referred to committee. But the country sided with Hayes, and with the aid of some Southern senators, the selections were finally confirmed. They earned praise as well as criticism. Hugh McCulloch, secretary of the Treasury for Lincoln and Johnson, who had disapproved of the Grant administration, was most favorably impressed: "The excellent judgment and independence you have displayed in the appointment of the members of your cabinet," he wrote, "have removed my apprehensions. . . . I am now more hopeful in regard to the future of the country . . . than I have been since the outbreak of the Civil War." Kenneth E. Davison called the cabinet the ablest presidential team between the Civil War and the twentieth century.

Hayes's next problem was that of patronage. As he said to Garfield, he was greatly embarrassed by the pressures to fill offices, especially since he was opposed to the spoils system and wanted to appoint only for vacancies. The resignation of David Davis had created an opening on the Supreme Court, to which he was anxious to elevate his friend Stanley Matthews, prominent Ohio lawyer, prosecutor, and judge, who had argued so successfully before the electoral commission not to go behind the returns and whose election to the Senate he had also favored. He had even told Garfield, who also wanted the Senate position, to stay in the House, where he was more definitely needed. Matthews's nomination to the Supreme Court was not sustained by the Senate, however, partially because of his prewar prosecution of W. B. Connelly, who had tried to help two fugitive slaves to escape, and because of his identification with various railroads. It was not until Garfield's administration that he was renominated and finally confirmed. The president had more luck with John Marshall Harlan, the Kentucky Republican he had originally wanted for attorney general, only to run into opposition from Senator Morton of Indiana. When in October he submitted Harlan's name to the Senate, he was successful. Harlan became a Supreme Court justice and went on to a notable career. Perhaps the most sensational of Hayes's appointments was that of Frederick Douglass, the country's foremost African American, as marshal for the District of Columbia. The conservative bar of the District was opposed, but many of the Republican newspapers welcomed this recognition of the famous black leader, who was then able to be sworn in and to enter upon his new office. To the renowned poet James Russell Lowell, Hayes offered either the Austrian or the Russian mission, although the poet eventually went to Spain; and he sent the author and translator Bayard Taylor to Germany; his friend Noyes to France; Edwin W. Stoughton, who had helped in Louisiana, to Russia; and the Philadelphia merchant and philanthropist John Welsh to Great Britain. Finally, in November 1878, he appointed Lincoln's former aide, future biographer and secretary of state, John Hay, assistant secretary of state.

The most difficult issue facing the new administration was the question of the removal of the troops from those Southern states where they had long protected Republican administrations. In Florida, the Democrats had already taken over, but in South Carolina and Louisiana, there were still two governments, with the Republican administrations dependent on the support of federal troops. Anxious to end sectional discord, Hayes was eager to conciliate the Southern whites while protecting the blacks. "Never did a President enter upon his duties with more sincere goodwill for every section," Ben Perley Poore remembered.

To accomplish his purposes, the president knew that he would have to withdraw the troops—Grant had already been willing to do so—but if he did it too soon, he would incur the ill will of a large number of Republicans in and out of Congress. Consequently, he sought compromises. As soon as the special session of Congress adjourned on March 18, the president and cabinet decided to deal with the question. Matthews, now senator from Ohio, and Evarts informed Daniel Chamberlain that Northern public opinion would no longer sustain the maintenance of troops to prop up Republican governments in the South; Hayes summoned both South Carolina governors, Chamberlain and Wade Hampton, who still claimed legitimacy, to Washington for consultation, and Hampton promised to respect the political and civil rights of the blacks even without the presence of federal troops. Although Chamberlain warned that the Republican party would be ruined in the South if the Democrats were allowed to have their way, a prediction that proved true, when the two rival governors left, Hayes determined to withdraw the troops from the statehouse, but not from the state lest he admit that they had been there without sanction of law. He did so on April 10, and Reconstruction in South Carolina came to an end. In spite of Hampton's promises, the returning conservatives—called Bourbons like the French monarchs—who never learned nor forgot anything, did not hesitate to gradually deprive the blacks of their rights.

In Louisiana there had long been two governments and judicial systems. In 1876 the Republicans had chosen Stephen B. Packard and the Democrats Francis T. Nicholls, both of whom claimed the governorship. Nicholls had already seized the supreme court and most organs of administration, while Packard was confined to the statehouse, where he and his legislature could maintain themselves only with the help of the federal troops. As he had already informed Chamberlain, Matthews now wrote to Packard that he could no longer count on federal military protection. To solve the problem, Hayes appointed a commission of five to make recommendations concerning the ending of federal intervention. The commission, consisting of four Republicans, one Democrat, and one independent, succeeded by various means, fair and foul, in persuading enough members of the Republican legislature to join its Democratic rival to give it a quorum. This body then counted Nicholls in and removed Packard. Thereupon, on April 20, Hayes ordered the troops to return to base camp from the statehouse, thus again leaving them in the state but abandoning the protection of the Packard government. In Louisiana, as in South Carolina, Reconstruction was over, and Nicholls's promises to safeguard black rights were as illusory as Hampton's. But the president was satisfied. "I now hope for peace," he wrote in his diary, "and what is more important, security and prosperity for the colored people. The result of my plans is to get from these States by their governors, legislatures, press, and people pledges that the Thirteenth, Fourteenth, and Fifteenth Amendments shall be faithfully observed; that the colored people shall have equal rights to labor, education, and the privileges of citizenship." He was confident that this was good work, but of course he was to be disappointed. Although he made efforts to cause blacks to be appointed to offices in the South—it would give them recognition and diminish race prejudice, he asserted—without federal interference the blacks' position, now that they were totally at the mercy of their racist former masters, would steadily deteriorate.

Of all of Hayes's actions, this surrender of Republican regimes in the South has been one of the most controversial. To be sure, some Republicans like the reformist writer Richard Henry Dana, Jr., were delighted and wrote him that they had not felt so hopeful for the country since Lee's surrender. But in Congress, Blaine severely condemned the abandonment of the Republican governors—if Packard, who had more votes than Hayes, was out, so was the president, he said, and many agreed with him. Ex-Senator Wade, who had seconded Hayes's nomination for president, was outraged. "You ask whether I remember what I said in favor of President Hayes in my endeavor to procure his nomination at the Cincinnati Convention," he wrote to Uriah H. Painter of the *New York Times*. "I do remember it, after what has since transpired, with indignation and a bitterness of soul that I never felt before. You know with what untiring zeal I labored for the emancipation of the slaves . . . and I supposed Governor Hayes was in full accord with me on that subject. But I have been deceived, betrayed, and even humiliated by the course he has taken." The hostile *New York Sun*, though not known for its interest in blacks' rights, not only kept harping on Hayes's failure to protect the blacks but also repeated Blaine's charge. Republican newspapers tended to welcome the end of strife with the South. "Within three days, the Southern question will disappear from federal politics," said the *New York Evening Post*, predicting that its disappearance would give even greater satisfaction to the people of the North than to those of the South, and the *Herald* praised Hayes for having redeemed his first and most important promise "so to govern as to abolish the South in a political sense." The more radical Republican journals, however, were critical, the *New York Times* calling the withdrawal a surrender. In fact, according to the historian James Ford Rhodes, within six weeks of his inauguration, Hayes had lost the support of his party.

But the president had little choice. His predecessor, General Grant, had decided to withdraw support from the disputed governments even before the inauguration, and the country was no longer ready to tolerate military interference in the South. As Ari Hoogenboom has stated so well, Hayes knew that Northern opinion would not long sustain the troops in the South, but from this weak

bargaining position he extracted from the rival Democratic governments promises to guarantee the voting and civil rights of all black
and white citizens. He was naive in accepting these pledges at face
value, but he had no viable option. This conclusion would seem to
be fully justified.

For Hayes, the Southern issue did not cease with the withdrawal
of the troops. Not only did he receive any number of outraged letters from Republicans who considered themselves betrayed, but in
July Thomas C. Anderson and other members of the Louisiana
returning board were charged with falsifying certain parish returns.
It was evident that the whole proceeding was directed against the
legitimacy of Hayes's title. Had the returning board found for Tilden,
Hayes mused, there would certainly not have been any prosecution.

Hayes's next problem was that of civil service reform. The spoils
system was so well established that the president's constitutional
power of appointing officers had been virtually eroded by the interference of senators, and Hayes was determined to restore executive powers. "Now for civil service reform," he wrote on April 22,
and embarked on a campaign that, while achieving partial success,
alienated him further from members of his party in Congress, many
of whom were convinced that patronage was the lifeblood of politics.
At the very first full cabinet meeting, on March 12, he appointed a
committee including Evarts and Schurz to draft a set of civil service
rules calling for examinations prior to hiring. On April 23, the secretary of the Treasury appointed a commission headed by John Jay,
the grandson of the first chief justice of the United States, well-
known abolitionist and New York lawyer, to examine the New York
Custom House. Collector Chester A. Arthur operated the office
efficiently, but it was totally controlled by Roscoe Conkling's political machine and thus offensive to Hayes because of his opposition
to machine politics in general and his rivalry with the New York
boss in particular. Although the president had to issue a call for a
special session of Congress to make the needed appropriation for
the army, which the previous Congress had omitted, on May 5 he

summoned Congress to meet only on October 15, thus leaving him time to deal with civil service reform without interference. Responding to the preliminary report of the Jay Commission on May 26, he stated that he concurred with its recommendations. He wanted the collection of revenues to be free from partisan control, to be operated exactly like a business. Party leaders were not to have any special influence over appointments, and he expressed his opposition to the participation of government employees in the management of election campaigns as well as their assessments for political purposes. On June 22, he issued an order to all federal officers calling attention to his letter to the secretary of the Treasury and his rule that no officer should take part in the management of political organizations, caucuses, conventions, or election campaigns. Their right to vote and to express their views on public questions was not to be denied, provided it did not interfere with the discharge of their official duties, and no assessment for political purposes on officers or subordinates was to be allowed.

It was Carl Schurz who most fully implemented these rules. Believing civil service reform to be his most important issue since slavery had been abolished, he sought to introduce it in the Department of the Interior, a collection of various bureaus long graft-ridden. To a great extent, he was successful, particularly in the Indian Bureau, notorious for its corruption. But in New York, Hayes's civil service rules were disregarded. In the office of the Collector of the Port, closely tied as it was to Roscoe Conkling's political machine, the naval officer, Alonzo B. Cornell, was the state Republican chairman, and he refused to give up either of his positions.

As the historian Robert Vance Bruce in his book, *1877: Year of Violence,* has pointed out, the late spring and summer of 1877 was a bad time for Hayes. In June Samuel Tilden appeared at the Manhattan Club in New York and delivered a talk harping on the alleged electoral fraud in seating his opponent. Then, before Hayes could continue his effort at civil service reform, his attention was taken up by the outbreak of strikes on the nation's major railroads. Driven to desperation by the railroads' repeated wage cuts, the last one of 10 percent, their employees seized trains and stations, and combined with miners to stage what amounted to the most general work stoppage in the nation's history, at the height of which some one hundred thousand men were out, six to seven thousand miles of tracks in their control. Serious riots occurred in Pittsburgh, Chicago, St. Louis, Martinsburg, Cumberland, Baltimore, and elsewhere, and Hayes was forced to respond to the request of state governors for federal aid against rebellion. He did so in response to West Virginia's governor's request on July 18, to Maryland's on July 21, and to Pennsylvania's on July 23, and issued proclamations admonishing all citizens against aiding or taking part in unlawful proceedings and calling on the strikers to disperse. To his satisfaction, the troops did not shed any blood; their appearance was sufficient to quell the disorders. Although sanctioned at the time, the government's interference on behalf of the employers can be severely criticized. However, the president himself was more sympathetic to the strikers than many of his contemporaries. Reflecting on the situation, he wrote in his diary, "The strikes have been put down by *force;* but now for the real remedy. Can't something be done by education of the strikers, by judicious control of the capitalists, by wise general policy to end or diminish the evil?" He thought the strikers were good men, but believed they had no right to interfere with the right to work of other people. As time went on, he would become more conscious of the injustices of workers' exploitation.

When the strikes were over, Hayes returned to his effort to reform the civil service. Following further reports of the Jay Commission, in September he asked Sherman to intimate to New York collector Chester A. Arthur, naval officer Alonzo B. Cornell, and surveyor George H. Sharpe that their resignations were desired. They refused, whereupon Hayes nominated Theodore Roosevelt, the later president's father; L. Bradford Prince, a prominent New York legislator, who had broken with Conkling during the 1876 presidential convention; and Edwin A. Merritt, who had been quartermaster general on Governor Reuben Fenton's staff, as their replacements. However, they would have to await the action of the Senate, where Roscoe Conkling was certain to oppose the dismantling of his New York machine since the appointees were generally opposed to him. As David M. Jordan has explained, "It came as a shock to old Washington hands to see a president directly challenge a leading senator on a matter of senatorial privilege like this. . . . The Senate's authority had not often been put to the test, and, when it had been, the Senate generally won." In Chicago, too, collector J. R. Jones refused to resign, whereupon Hayes suspended him and appointed his friend William H. Smith in his stead.

Conkling's counterattack followed in short order. At the Rochester, New York, state Republican convention late in September, he not only arranged for the defeat of George William Curtis's resolution upholding the president but also for the adoption of a civil service plank asserting the right of officeholders to retain their jobs. "When Dr. Johnson defined patriotism as the last refuge of a scoundrel," he said in an uncompromising speech, "he was unconscious of the then undeveloped capabilities and uses of the word reform." Charles Foster, the Ohio politician who had been present at the Wormley Hotel Conference, wrote, "Conkling has taken a decided stand against your Administration and you must assume that he means to fight," suggesting that Hayes do nothing in malice and that the country was behind him. The Ohio election occurred soon afterward, and it too resulted in a defeat for the president's supporters. That these results would cause loss of friends and the encouragement of enemies was obvious.

Thus, when Congress opened on October 15, Hayes had already been considerably weakened. "I am satisfied that his six months administration have partially blinded the President to the danger and criticisms of his course. It seems to be impossible for the President to see through the atmosphere of praise in which he lives," Garfield commented. The lack of harmony between Hayes and his party was indeed common knowledge, and his message to the special session did nothing to correct it. Calling for the funds necessary for the upkeep of the armed forces, which had not been paid for months, he also requested support for the American delegates to the 1878 Paris Exhibition of Agriculture, Industry, and Fine Arts. He pointed out that the invitation to participate in this event had been communicated by the French minister in May 1876, and that the Department of State had received official advice of the strong desire of the French government that the United States participate in the exhibit. In addition, Hayes recalled that the government of Sweden-Norway had addressed an official invitation to the United States to take part in the Stockholm International Prison Congress, for which a joint congressional resolution had authorized the appointment of a commissioner in 1875. An appropriation of eight thousand dollars to meet the commissioner's expenses had then been made, but the Swedish government had postponed the congress till 1878, and Hayes had renewed the commission. He now asked for a reappropriation of that sum. Congress did pass the appropriations, but the House, disregarding the vague promises made to Garfield in various negotiations during the disputed election campaign, elected Samuel J. Randall speaker. As the *New York Sun* gleefully reported, a Republican caucus determined that appointees to judicial positions discharge Republican regulations of the past ten years. The caucus also decided to ask the president to select Republicans for those positions in the South where any party members were left, and proposed that a committee be appointed to wait upon Hayes to point out his errors to him.

The House continued to defy the president. It passed the inflationary Bland Silver Bill, creating a silver currency with a 412.5-grain silver dollar, as well as the repeal of the Resumption Act of 1875, measures to which Hayes was inalterably opposed. And the animadversion to the administration was by no means merely a Democratic one. As Hayes realized and confided to his diary, "It is now obvious that there is a very decided opposition to the Administration in both houses of Congress among the Republican members. . . . The objections extend to all of my principal acts." He thought it applied to the cabinet, particularly to Evarts and Schurz, who were unpopular as alleged disorganizers, as well as to Key, who was disliked as a Democrat. It also concerned the civil service reforms, which allegedly stripped Congress of all control of the patronage, and the Southern policy as a departure from Republican ideals. Hayes's alienation from the party continued to be a problem throughout his term of office.

His political difficulties did not keep Hayes from traveling frequently to various parts of the country. In June he went to New England, where he received an honorary degree from Harvard; in August he visited New England again, stopping at his ancestral towns in Vermont, and in September he undertook a trip to the South to see how his policy had worked there. After going home to Ohio, he traveled to Kentucky, Tennessee, Georgia, and Virginia delivering forceful speeches and was pleased to be heartily received everywhere. "The trip South has been the greatest success as it has been the most pleasant surprise of the year," commented William H. Smith, who was especially impressed with the president's addresses. In November Hayes went south once more, this time to Richmond, where he again mistakenly thought that there were thousands of people who would like to unite with the conservative Republicans of the North. Seemingly oblivious to the constant criticisms of his travels by the *New York Sun*, which continually published his portrait with the word FRAUD printed on his forehead, he was more than satisfied with the seeming success of his Southern policy, even its acceptance by Southern blacks. Addressing a group of them in Atlanta, he told them that their interests were better protected if the great mass of intelligent whites were left alone by the government, and tried to prove it by maintaining that there had been fewer outrages during the past six months than ever before. Of course, this analysis was misleading, but he never lost his optimism about the improvement of Southern racial problems.

During the hot summer months, when not away from Washington, the president moved to the Soldiers' Home, then outside the city. It offered some relief from the heat of the capital, and Hayes took some time out to have a bust portrait of himself painted by the artist Carl Brown. He considered it the best likeness yet.

Nevertheless, Hayes enjoyed living in the White House, which Lucy was doing a good job of refurbishing. The family acquired a new piano, and according to Emily Apt Geer, Lucy's biographer, it was during her stay that the old copper bathtubs were removed and new bathrooms with running water installed. A telephone was also put into the executive mansion. Frequent entertainments contributed to Lucy's excellent reputation, and her husband was delighted that her lively sympathy for all around her had made her intensely popular. As far as he was concerned, he had hardly moved in when he invited his ex-Confederate friend Guy Bryan to come and see him. The visit not only pleased him for the sake of his long-standing friendship with Bryan but also as an example of his effort to end controversies between North and South. Immediately after a dinner for a son of the Russian tsar where wine punch was served, Lucy's ban on alcohol, later winning her the name of "Lemonade Lucy," went into effect as part of the White House cuisine, much to the gratification of temperance advocates. The president, not a total abstainer at first, became one in order to set an example to the country.

The most noteworthy entertainment occurred on the occasion of the presidential couple's silver anniversary. On that day, December 30, 1877, members of the family, including the minister who had performed the original ceremony, gathered in the mansion. On the next day, a great reception took place in a splendidly decorated White House trimmed with bunting and running vines. Members of the cabinet and their wives, old friends from Ohio, delegates from the Twenty-third Regiment, and others were invited. At nine the band intoned Mendelssohn's "Wedding March," and the couple, followed by the family, came downstairs to go to the East Room and greet the guests. Lucy, resplendent in a white silk dress with draperies of white brocade, each headed with two rows of tasseled fringes and with a full plaiting at the sides, was a greatly admired hostess. It was the first time such an event had ever taken place in the White House.

The regular session of the Forty-fifth Congress began on December 3. Repeating many of the points he had made previously, the president, again emphasizing his efforts at pacification in the South, maintained that the withdrawal of the troops had been successful in establishing peace. "No unprejudiced mind will deny that the terrible and often fatal collisions which for several years have been of frequent occurrence and have agitated and alarmed the public mind have almost entirely ceased, and that a spirit of mutual forbearance and hearty national interest has succeeded," he asserted. At the same time, he reiterated his desire to protect the rights of Southern blacks. As he put it, "It should be our fixed and unalterable determination to protect by all available and proper means under the Constitution and the laws the lately emancipated race in the enjoyment of their rights and privileges, and I urge upon those who to whom heretofore the colored people have sustained the relation of bondmen the wisdom and justice of humane and liberal local legislation with respect to their education and general welfare." He endorsed conservative financial measures, strongly advocated the resumption of specie payments, and made clear his conviction that the value of a silver coin must be equal to gold. Civil service reform, the preservation of forests, aid to states for education, and efforts to assimilate Indians came next, as did an optimistic review of foreign relations.

Although he received merited praise for the message from various parts of the country, Garfield calling it able and particularly strong on the financial question and others terming it one of the most statesmanlike papers issued in Washington since the days of

John Quincy Adams, Congress continued its independent policies. Conkling was successful in blocking the confirmation of Roosevelt and Prince to take the places of collector Arthur and naval officer Cornell (as surveyor Sharpe's term was up, his successor, General Edwin A. Merritt, was confirmed). Hayes, however, remained undaunted. "My New York nominations were rejected, thirty-one to twenty-five," he commented. "But the end is not yet. I am right, and shall not give up the contest." Then he went to New York to attend the Union League reception, the opening of the Museum of Natural History, and the New England dinner.

Further trouble with Congress could not be avoided. The Senate joined the House in passing the silver bill, though Senator William B. Allison had weakened it by an amendment restricting the purchase of silver to two to four million dollars per month. Hayes vetoed the measure on February 28, declaring that "it is my firm conviction that if the country is to be benefited by a silver coinage it can be done by the issue of silver dollars of full value. A currency worth less than it purports to be worth will in the end defraud not only creditors, but all who are engaged in legitimate business, and none more surely than those who are dependent on their daily labor for their daily bread." However, Congress overrode his objections on the same day. Although it did pass the appropriations for the exhibitions, the president's estrangement from his party was highlighted by a manifesto to New Hampshire Republicans by William E. Chandler charging Hayes with the conclusion of a corrupt bargain with the Democrats to secure office by promising to relax Northern control of the South. "He has pursued a suicidal policy toward Congress and is almost without a friend," commented Garfield at the time of the veto of the silver bill.

And yet, Hayes was not unpopular. True, in January 1878, there was even talk of impeaching the president, and not only Chandler but Montgomery Blair, Lincoln's postmaster general, also attacked him, as Ari Hoogenboom has pointed out, though at the same time General H. V. Boynton of the *Cincinnati Gazette* vigorously defended him. As the *Chicago Times* facetiously rhymed, "The Chandler's red glare, the Blairs bursting in air, disclose through the night that R. B. is still there." An endorsement of the administration that month by the New Hampshire legislature showed that Chandler's letter had not done Hayes any harm, even in the politician's home state, and Southerners continued to praise him for having pacified the section. At any rate, he remained undisturbed. Expressing his satisfaction with his accomplishments on the first anniversary of his taking office, he thought his general course had been correct. Though he realized that "a nonpartisan President or Administration," as he called it, would be feebly supported in Congress or by the press, he believed that he had succeeded in establishing peace in the South and in upholding order during the strikes without causing any casualties. Civil service reforms, a vigorous policy toward Mexico, and making important and useful appointments to various offices, also seemed to him to be matters of pride.

He usually spent his days in an orderly sequence. Rising at seven, he wrote until breakfast at about 8:30. Then came prayers and the reading of a chapter of the Bible, each one present reading a verse in turn, and all kneeling to repeat the Lord's Prayer. More writing and arranging business followed until ten, with the next two hours in the cabinet room to receive visitors. He set aside noon to two on Tuesdays and Fridays for cabinet meetings, with the same time for business callers on other days. Lunching at two, he then took care of his correspondence, and at 3:30 took a drive for an hour and a half. After a short nap, he had dinner at six, followed by the reception of callers until about 10:30 or 11:30. But he felt that he did not have enough exercise. To compensate, he engaged in gymnastics before getting dressed, walked rapidly for ten minutes after each meal, went horseback riding regularly with Secretary Sherman, and ate and drank coffee and tea in moderation.

Further difficulties arose in connection with the Louisiana case against Thomas C. Anderson, the only defendant to be tried for tampering with parish returns. After a state judge refused to grant a transfer to a federal court in January, the proceedings started. Anderson was found guilty, sentenced to two years in prison, but with a recommendation for mercy. On March 18, the Louisiana supreme court set the verdict aside on the grounds that when committed, the offense had not been a crime. Nevertheless, it was embarrassing for Hayes. "Anderson has gone, Hayes must follow," wrote the Democratic press, though the president was convinced the whole matter was a political vendetta of the Bourbons. But soon he had to face a more serious problem. Not only did Republican Senator Timothy Otis Howe deliver a speech in Congress castigating him for having abandoned Governor Packard—Hayes thought Howe was miffed because he was not appointed to the Supreme Court—but on May 13, Congressman Clarkson N. Potter, a New York Democrat, introduced a resolution to investigate alleged frauds in Florida and Louisiana during the recent presidential vote. The resolution passed, and as Hayes fully realized, it was intended to reverse the result of the election. If sustained, it would cause another rebellion, he surmised, and at Gettysburg, on Decoration Day, he made it quite clear that he would resist any effort to replace him. If Tilden tried to take over the presidency, he said to a brother of his friend John Herron, he would be arrested and shot. A reporter from the *Philadelphia Times* overheard the conversation and the paper published it. This unauthorized revelation caused great excitement.

Although the Potter Committee investigation started with great fanfare, in the long run it disappointed its sponsors. On June 14, Representative Horatio C. Burchard of Illinois introduced a resolution that stated:

Whereas the joint meeting of the two Houses of the Fortieth Congress convened pursuant to law and the Constitution for the purpose of ascertaining and counting the votes for President and Vice President for the term commencing March 4, 1877, upon counting the votes Rutherford B. Hayes was declared to be elected President and William A. Wheeler was declared elected Vice President for the same term; therefore . . . no subsequent Congress and neither House has jurisdiction to revise the action at such joint meeting, and any attempt by either House to annul or disregard such action on the title to office arising therefrom would be revolutionary and is disapproved by this House.

The resolution passed, and the immediate threat to Hayes's title was over. To the committee's request that he furnish an alleged letter promising a position to the election supervisor of one of the Louisiana parishes if he favored the Republicans he replied that he had no recollection of any such letter and none such were in his files. The effort to prove that the Republicans won by bribery then backfired when in October 1878 the New York newspapers published the so-called cipher dispatches, which showed that the Democrats, particularly Tilden's nephew, Colonel William T. Pelton, were deeply involved in efforts to bribe Southern returning boards. Tilden denied any knowledge of the dispatches, but when at the end of the session the majority of the Potter Committee issued a lengthy report maintaining that Tilden was entitled to the electoral votes of Florida and Louisiana, omitting any mention of the cipher dispatches, the minority highlighted them, and the Democrats' attack on the legitimacy of the presidency failed completely.

After Congress adjourned on June 20, Hayes, in accordance with the Tenure of Office Act, suspended Arthur and Cornell and appointed Merritt, the surveyor, and Cornell's deputy, S. W. Burt, in their stead. It was obvious that in view of Conkling's opposition in the next session of the Senate the president would have a tough struggle to secure the confirmation of these appointments.

The president continued his frequent travels. On Decoration Day, while Lucy was in the Adirondacks with Vice President Wheeler, he went to Gettysburg and stayed with Edward McPherson, the former clerk of the House, whom he had appointed to head the Bureau of Engraving and Printing. On a trip to West Point for commencement exercises he took a boat trip up the Hudson River and enjoyed the great scenery. He also visited Mount Vernon, attended the centennial of the Wyoming Massacre in Pennsylvania, and returned to Ohio. In September he undertook a trip to the Midwest, Chicago and St. Paul, a journey he considered, again, the most happy, useful, and successful excursion he had ever made. Immediately afterward, he was present at the New York session of the board of trustees of the Peabody Fund for the education of Southern blacks, a charity with which he would remain connected for many years, and later in the fall, he went to Montpelier, Virginia, to visit Madison's home, traveled to Cumberland, Maryland, and home to Ohio once again.

The midterm elections showed several Republican gains in the North, while the South was now solidly Democratic. But the administration had already suffered a setback because it had become evident that after March 4 the Senate as well as the House would be Democratic. Although Hayes thought public opinion more friendly, constant attacks on his "fraudulency" had their effect. The *New York Sun* even regretted that the president was not Jewish so that he would have to make restitution on the Day of Atonement. Conkling, still bitterly opposed to the president he now called "Rutherfraud," expressed the opinion that Hayes would be deposed if both houses became Democratic. Of course, his prediction proved to be incorrect. The two Democratic houses met and made no attempt to change the results of the 1876 vote.

Hayes expressed satisfaction with the election results. With his usual optimism, despite the earlier loss of the Senate, he thought the outcome gratifying because of Republican strength in the North. He was especially pleased about the defeat of Benjamin Butler in Massachusetts, whom he considered "the most dangerous and wicked demagogue" the country had ever had, and since Butler, a much feared political manipulator, had been unable to exert influence upon the administration, he had indeed turned violently against it. But Hayes did regret the solid opposition against the Republicans in the South. The answer, he thought, was an effort to induce whites to join two parties instead of merely one.

When Congress convened on December 2 he delivered his second annual message. Brief as usual, it began with an assertion that the country was at peace with all nations, the public credit stronger than ever before and economic conditions improving. Then he turned to the devastation caused by a yellow fever epidemic in the South and recommended the establishment of a national sanitary administration. A consideration of the failure of South Carolina and Louisiana and several other Southern election districts to live up to their promises to enforce the Civil War amendments and protect the rights of blacks followed, and he vowed that whatever authority rested with him he would not hesitate to put forth to this end. He praised the condition of the Treasury, cautioned against any changes in the existing financial legislation—the resumption of specie payments—and went on to consider the reports of the various cabinet departments. Strongly supporting the attempt to induce the Indians to settle down as farmers, he called for justice for the "aborigines," endorsed the conservation of natural resources, pleaded for strong support for agriculture, and gave an optimistic review of relations with foreign nations.

The message was generally well received, although the usual objections of Democrats and dissatisfied Republicans could not be muted. Calling the document ineffective, the *New York Times* faulted the president for not presenting an indictment that would have fastened upon the South the odium it so richly deserved, and the *Sun* again castigated him for failing to make any new suggestions "worthy of a man of affairs" and showing himself "to be as incompetent as he is a Fraudulent President."

Hayes's unfinished business with Congress was still the confirmation of his appointments to the New York Custom House. He knew that it would be difficult to prevail against Conkling's invocation of senatorial courtesy, but he was confident of overcoming the New Yorker. He was not mistaken. After he sent a message to the Senate accusing Arthur and Cornell of conducting their offices as part of the political machinery under their control and arguing that the collectorship should be conducted like a business, on February 4 that body, some fifteen Republicans voting aye, confirmed the surveyor Merritt in place of Arthur and Cornell's deputy, S. W. Burt, in place of Cornell, giving Hayes one of his most remarkable successes. His civil service reform efforts had at least partially prevailed.

At the end of the year the president briefly traveled to New York for a memorial for the poet William Cullen Bryant, who had died in June. When he returned he was able to chalk up two more victories that winter. On January 1, specie resumption succeeded better than anyone had expected. Now that greenbacks could be exchanged freely for gold, no effort was made to do so. Of the $346 million in notes outstanding only $130,000 were presented, and the paper money question was settled. As Hayes had been a steady supporter of the measure, he could take considerable satisfaction in its success. Then came a skillful handling of the problem of Chinese immigration. Because of nativist feelings in the West, Congress had passed a bill restricting Chinese entry to the United States, a clear violation of the Burlingame Treaty with the Chinese empire, which extended to the Chinese all the rights of immigration of the most favored nations. In spite of strong pressure to sign the measure, Hayes, calling attention to the inappropriateness of abrogating a treaty without specific cause and to the consequences such actions would entail to Americans in China, particularly merchants and missionaries, vetoed the bill. The reaction from various parts of the country, largely outside of the West, was mostly favorable, and correspondents praised the president for having upheld the American ideal of the equality of all men. In addition, he signed the Arrears of Pensions Bill passed in January, awarding pensions to veterans dating from their day of death, disability, or discharge. Its great cost caused many opponents to hope for a veto, but Hayes, convinced that it was right, and always open to aid his former comrades, signed it without hesitation.

In his conduct of foreign affairs, Hayes was also successful. Difficulties with Mexico arose following the assumption of power by Porfirio Diaz. Because of the undemocratic nature of Diaz's accession and questions about his ability to pacify the border, Hayes refused to recognize him. Marauding bands along the Rio Grande induced Secretary of War McCrary to issue an order permitting General Edward O. C. Ord to continue pursuit into Mexican territory if necessary, a highly controversial measure that gave the opposition an opportunity to attack the administration it hated. After charging that the general had been given power to start a war in order to conciliate the Southern vote, the *New York Sun* lambasted "the cunning device of Mexican annexation by which Mr. Hayes and Mr. Evarts hope and expect to draw away public attention from the fraudulent title by which they hold their present posts." Eventually, cooperation with the Mexican government managed to settle the border problems, and in the spring of 1878 the Diaz government was recognized. Thus matters were settled peacefully in spite of opposition charges that Hayes was eager to start a war with the neighboring country. In November 1878, arbitrating a dispute between Argentina and Paraguay, the administration awarded the territory between Pilcomayo and the Verde River to Paraguay, so that a whole department of that country was called Presidente Hayes and its capital named after him. He discharged the outstanding debt of $5.5 million to Great Britain under the Halifax fishery assessment agreed upon by the Treaty of Washington, settling the wartime Alabama claims, and established good relations with the major powers of Europe.

Hayes's Indian policy, for which Secretary of the Interior Carl Schurz was responsible, was marked by attempts to treat the Indians fairly. Schurz's success in preventing the takeover of the Indian Bureau by the War Department prevented excessive military action against the native Americans, but during the first years of the administration, several Indian wars could not be prevented. In 1877 the Nez Percé, led by Chief Joseph, conducted a remarkable retreat of some one thousand miles to the Canadian border, where they were defeated by General Nelson A. Miles; then the Bannocks rose, harassed by the seizure of their lands; and finally the Northern Cheyenne became belligerent. Schurz attempted to carry out a policy of severalty, with detribalization causing the Indians to acquire land individually and settle down to a life like that of whites, and he established schools for their training. While this effort of assimilation tended to destroy Indian culture, it was infinitely better than the army's idea that the only good Indian was a dead Indian.

All in all, the first two years of the Hayes administration were more successful than could have been expected after the disputed election. As the *Atlantic Monthly* pointed out, interference in state elections had been abandoned, financial obligations vindicated, burdens of taxation lifted, and national credit secured. The periodical also praised the reform of the civil service and gave it credit for Republican victories achieved in the fall elections. To be sure, the president had earned the enmity of members of his own party, but his popularity in the country at large had grown. "It gives me pleasure to congratulate you upon the impartial manner in which you have honorably conducted public affairs of the country since your election to the chair as President of the United States," one Virginian wrote him late in the fall of 1879. "Simplicity and firmness of character tempered with just and benevolent principles have produced among the citizens of the Commonwealth kind and generous feelings for you. It is an honor to us to have such a true and good magistrate at the head of public affairs." Many others shared this sentiment.

# 6

---

# The Presidency:
# Last Two Years

The second half of Hayes's presidency was marked by much less trouble with his party than the first. Relations with Congress may have been more difficult—after all, both Houses were in the hands of the Democrats—but Hayes prevailed in his struggles with the opposition. The result was to be a Republican victory in 1880.

Hayes was now fifty-seven years old. Still vigorous, well liked by those around him, he continued to make an excellent impression as a healthy, kindly gentleman. Accompanied by his attractive and elegant wife, he was able to overcome various political enmities and maintained good social relations with such opponents as Senators Thurman and Pendleton. In spite of his great desire for sectional pacification, he was unwilling to countenance the repeal of the federal election laws and was now ready to deal with the Democratic Congress.

Because at the time of its adjournment on March 4, 1879, the Forty-fifth Congress had not made any appropriations for the legislative, executive, and judicial expenses of the government, including the costs of the armed forces, Hayes immediately called its successor into special session for March 18. The reason for this lack of action was the effort of the Democrats to repeal federal supervision of elections by attaching riders to the appropriation bills, thus preventing the enforcement of the Thirteenth, Fourteenth, and Fifteenth amendments passed during and after the Civil War. The Republican Senate had refused to go along with the Democratic House in these efforts, so that no appropriations were passed. But with the Democratic capture of the Senate, only the president could still preserve these Civil War gains. Moreover, the powers of the presidency itself were at stake. Considering the riders an evasion of the constitutional rights of the president to participate in legislation and determined not to yield to unwanted measures contained in riders, he found it easy to deny rumors that he might weaken. "I don't like Democratic attempts to revolutionize the Gov't of our fathers," he wrote to William Dean Howells, while confiding to his diary that he could not consent to the repeal of election laws enacted by Congress unless others equally effective were substituted.

His stance was popular in the North. Garfield, who had heard reports that Hayes was weakening, was pleased to hear that he was firm and determined. Former Governor Dennison was equally reassured: "We are all delighted with the firmness of the President . . . in his intended resistance to the rebel purposes of the majority of Congress," he wrote. Hayes did not disappoint his supporters.

True to his intentions, when Congress met, he sent a message asking for the necessary appropriations. For brevity the message had perhaps never before been equaled, noted the Havana, New York, *Journal*, but "from its directness and pith will hereafter always be cited as a model." In spite of lengthy debates, however, Congress did not heed the president and on April 25 passed an army appropriation bill with a rider repealing the section allowing federal troops to keep the peace at the polls. In accordance with his long consideration of his duties and rights in the matter, Hayes promptly vetoed the measure. "The enactment of this bill into law will establish a precedent which will tend to destroy the equal independence of the several branches of the Government," he stated. "Its principle places not merely the Senate, and the Executive, but the judiciary also, under the coercive direction of the House." His veto was upheld, and congratulations poured in from correspondents all over the country. "It places the Republican party on the vantage ground, and restores you to the confidence of the doubting ones," a Cincinnati friend wrote to him.

Congress's next move, on May 9, was a bill to prohibit military interference at elections. As this was again an effort to annul federal powers to enforce civil rights, the president issued another ringing veto, citing numerous historical precedents for the sections to be annulled. "Under the sweeping terms of the bill, the National Government is effectually shut out from the exercise of the right and from the discharge of the imperative duty to use its whole executive power whenever and wherever required for the enforcement of its laws at the places and times when and where its elections are held," he wrote in what Garfield called by far the ablest paper he had ever produced. Hayes prevailed again.

But the fight was far from over. Within a few weeks, Congress passed another appropriations act for legislative, executive, and judicial expenses, which again contained riders repealing parts of the Enforcement Acts authorizing the appointment of federal supervisors and marshals for elections. In a strongly worded veto regretting the failure of Congress to heed his previous objections to riders, on May 29 Hayes once more expressed his disapproval, remarking that "the object of the bill is to destroy any control whatever by the United States over the Congressional elections," and the veto was again upheld.

On June 23, declaring that though he was willing to concur on suitable amendments to the election laws he could not consent to their absolute repeal, Hayes sent in another veto, this time of a judicial appropriations bill. Congress now tried to annul federal interference by prohibiting the compensation of federal officials at election time, and his veto was once again upheld, as was his disapproval on June 30 of a bill for the payment of United States marshals with a rider prohibiting payment to those employed at elections. He did approve a legislative appropriation bill on June 23 that did not contain any objectionable riders, but by and large he had been eminently successful in his struggle with Congress, which adjourned on July 1.

During this entire contest, Hayes continued to carry on his lively social life. Entertaining members of the cabinet, the Supreme Court, Congress, friends, and relatives, he gave frequent dinners, was delighted with Lucy's social skills, and noted that her popularity was ever increasing. "Her large warm heart and lively sympathy for or with all around her, with a fair share of beauty and talents" made this possible, he wrote. Loyal to old friends, he appointed Guy Bryan a visitor to West Point, as a member of a board reporting annually to the secretary of war, but the Texan was unable to accept the honor. Hayes's children were doing well: Webb was still with him at the White House, Birch had a law practice in Toledo, Ruddy was in college, and Scott and Fanny lived in the mansion. A good family man, the president still felt lonely whenever his wife was absent and enjoyed the presence of his children. Also fond of his animals, in his diary he even noted the death of his wartime horse, Old Whitey.

A soon as Congress adjourned, Hayes, in need of well-merited relaxation, embarked on a voyage down the Potomac on the U.S. steamboat *Tallapoosa*. Accompanied by members of the cabinet, friends, Webb, and Ruddy, he visited Fortress Monroe, sailed into the open ocean for a few hours and, on the way back, stopped at Washington's birthplace. It was a rewarding trip.

In the meantime, a number of pardoning issues came up. A board appointed to reexamine the conviction of General Fitz-John Porter came to the conclusion that he ought to be restored to full rank, a report Hayes promptly sent to Congress. He himself was not sure what to do in the matter—he was not opposed to clemency, but, sympathizing with his friend Pope, felt that on the merits of the case Porter had no claims—and the report was not fully acted

upon until he was out of office. Another question was the pardoning of purveyors of allegedly pornographic material. Hayes par-
doned Ezra Hervey Heywood of the New England Free Love
League, who had been fined for one of his publications, because
though disapproving, as Ari Hoogenboom has shown, he did not
consider the works criminal. In the case of Robigne Mortimer Ben-
nett, who had sent through the mail a book on free love, the president, again totally disagreeing with the main premises of the work,
wondered whether in view of the fact that the publication had not
been considered a crime in Massachusetts and New York at the
time of its appearance a pardon was not again in order. In the end,
however, on the grounds that he did not wish to interfere with the
Department of Justice, he decided against it.

Because of his strong stand against congressional interference,
Hayes's reputation had greatly improved since the previous year,
and to some extent he restored good relations with the greater por-
tion of the Republican party in Congress. According to Benjamin
Perley Poore, "His pure patriotism, his high rectitude of intentions,
and his personal virtues had never been in doubt, and when he was
again found acting in accord with the party that elected him, it was
believed that he would be carried pleasantly through his embarrassing duties and that his civil success would match his exploits in
arms." Summing up the special session called by the executive in
1879, by castigating the Democrats, the *New York Evening Post*
pointed out, "They did not count on so stubborn a resistance as the
President has made. They had so often described him as a poor
creature without a mind of his own that they had come themselves
to believe what they said." Correspondents compared his stand to
that of Governor Morton of Indiana during the war, when Morton
went to the banks to obtain money the legislature had not voted. A
Richmond observer, J. L. M. Curry, thought Hayes's state papers
admirable and that he might well rest his fame as a statesman on his
letter of acceptance and the civil service regulations. He expressed

his regret that Hayes would not run for a second term, assuring him that people north and south, east and west approved of his political course. Others, too, were critical of his decision not to run again; a Bostonian assured him that in spite of the endorsement of Grant by the *Boston Journal*, Hayes was the best man for the office. "It certainly does rejoice my heart to know that the best men of all parties in this section speak so kindly of you and I know the people are with you as they have been with but few if any who have occupied your position."

In spite of all this praise, the president was somewhat dubious about the advantages of his tenure of power. Though realizing that the presidency had many attractions and enjoyments, he was tired of this "life of bondage, responsibility, and toil." Wishing the term were over, he rejoiced that it was only going to last a year and a half longer. In the meantime, he continued to acquire portraits of his predecessors to decorate the White House.

In September, Hayes set out on his travels again. Accompanied by Lucy, Birchard, Scott, Fanny, General Sherman, and others, he went to Cincinnati, Detroit, and then to the West, to Kansas, where he visited the state fair at Neosho. At Fort Leavenworth, he spent time with General Pope and returned via Illinois, Indiana (where there was another state fair), and Ohio. These journeys were more than mere pleasure trips. Speaking frequently, he advocated his policies, took credit for an improvement of the economy, and repeated his refusal to seek a second term. At Greenfield, Ohio, he predicted that business would soon pick up, a theme he repeated in Detroit, and again at Lincoln's home in Springfield, where, in what one observer called "a capital speech," he encouraged businessmen by taking credit for the imminent end of the recession. It was exactly what the country needed, commented the *New York Evening Post*. Accompanied by Governor Shelby M. Cullom and his wife, he paid his respects at Lincoln's tomb, which he found most impressive. When he reached his home at Spiegel Grove, he met with the trustees of the Birchard Library and offered to assume its indebtedness of fourteen thousand dollars in return for a tract in Toledo. Even though this transaction would cost him a considerable sum of money, he was anxious to see the library in good condition as a monument to his uncle. On Thanksgiving he was in Philadelphia at the home of Bishop Matthew Simpson, where he met his family, which had preceded him. Visiting Philadelphia again at the end of the year he encountered General Grant, who was on his way to Washington where he promised to call on Lucy, which he did.

The fall elections in 1879 seemed to be a general endorsement of the Republicans. Hayes was pleased, especially with the successes in Ohio, where among other victories the Republicans elected Charles Foster governor on a hard-money platform, a result he interpreted as an approval of the administration's policy about appropriations. The November elections were equally encouraging, although in New York Conkling had seen to it that Cornell was nominated and elected governor. Yet in spite of Cornell's victory, the defeat of Lucius Robinson, Tilden's protégé, was a source of satisfaction to the president, and the Republican victories were indeed widely seen as a sanction of the administration's policies during the special session.

In his message to the first regular session of the Forty-sixth Congress on December 1, Hayes took credit for the revival of business following the successful completion of the resumption of specie payments, discussed his civil service reforms at great length, and spoke against polygamy in Utah. He also praised the efforts to settle the Indians upon farm lots and took pride in the diplomatic successes of the administration. He was proud of the successes in efforts to arrest the depredations on the timberlands of the United States, urged the enlargement of the facilities of the Department of Agriculture, and expressed his gratification that educational privileges had been advanced throughout the year. Always interested in libraries, he recommended proper accommodations for the Library of Congress and for improvements in the District of Columbia. The reaction to it was the usual one, Republicans praising it as "the strongest state paper published in many a day," and Democrats deriding it as "destitute of any great suggestions on any subject whatever."

The president often had trouble with his appointments. Among others, the Senate not only failed to confirm his choice of Governor Morton's son for collector in San Francisco, but it could and did question the sincerity of his commitment to civil service reform because from time to time he himself did not hesitate to nominate friends and politicians who had been useful to him. Nevertheless, when he nominated Secretary of War McCrary for U. S. circuit judge, the secretary was speedily confirmed, as was his chosen successor, Governor Alexander Ramsey of Minnesota. The Senate also gave its consent to the president's appointment of the Tennessee loyalist Horace Maynard as postmaster general, in place of Key, who became a U. S. district court judge in Tennessee. Otherwise Congress, dominated by the opposition, was difficult to handle. It even steadfastly refused to follow Secretary of the Treasury Sherman's recommendation to strike from the greenbacks the inscription designating them legal tender.

The last year of Hayes's presidency was not very different from the preceding one. The difficulties with Congress about riders and appointments, senatorial courtesy being again invoked, were reminiscent of the previous struggle. And the president realized that his Southern policy was not as successful as he had expected. The failure of the Bourbons to grant equal rights to blacks troubled him, as he acknowledged in his annual message, and in April he was visited by black delegates complaining about their deprivation of political rights, even in the border state of Missouri, where their voting strength was not reflected by representation in state offices. All he could say in reply was that he had urged all federal officers to see to it that blacks be given the offices to which they were entitled. As for Hayes, he was eagerly awaiting his release from office. "I am now in my last year of the Presidency and look forward to its close as a schoolboy longs for the coming vacation," he wrote to Bryan. He had expressed similar feelings about the governorship; whether he was quite honest with himself is questionable.

One of the questions Hayes had raised in his December 1879 message was the problem of the governorship of Utah. The territory was large enough to merit admission as a state, but the issue of polygamy was in the way. Anxious as he was to end the dominance of the Mormon Church in the area—he hoped that the laws against the practice of plural marriage would be enforced now that the Supreme Court had held them constitutional, he was unable to prevail. The problem would not be solved until the 1890s.

He again made the White House, for which he had steadily collected portraits of his predecessors, the center of splendid entertainments, starting out with the usual New Year's reception, which was unfortunately marred by an untoward incident. An appointee who had not been confirmed walked up to the president and threatened that if Providence inflicted as much disgrace and poverty on Hayes as on him, the president would not have a happy moment for the rest of his life. The unlucky appointee, Henry De Alma, had been sent to Sitka, Alaska, and when his confirmation failed, had had to come back at his own expense. He had been given a sum of money in compensation but found it insufficient. "Here we have a very small would-be despot," he shouted as he was ushered out, not realizing that the president had no part in confirmations. The reception then proceeded with the usual success. A less interrupted affair took place two weeks later when officeholders, millionaires, and others were entertained in flower-decorated rooms, and on February 11, a diplomatic reception became the most brilliant event of the season.

On the occasion of the third anniversary of his assumption to power, Hayes reflected on his record. "The past has been on the whole, as I look back, more satisfactory than I hoped it would be," he wrote. To Bryan, he wrote that he was not without pride in the results attained. Mentioning the foreign service, the judiciary, and the Indian policy, he asserted that in Washington, the government was never better served. Naturally, to his old Confederate friend, he boasted about his appointment of many Southern Democrats.

In April, the family suffered a deep loss when Dr. Joseph T. Webb died. Lucy's brother had been Rud's good wartime comrade; he was a skillful physician who had been popular in the army, a man fond of sports and of excellent good humor. In later years, he suffered both physical and mental ills, and died of apoplexy in Minneapolis. Lucy went immediately to Minnesota to bring back his remains for burial in Cincinnati. Both the president and Lucy missed him dearly.

It was not long before Hayes had to engage again in a struggle about riders. On May 4, Congress passed another appropriations bill for the payment of federal marshals, again prohibiting payment to them for duties at elections. As he had done before, the president promptly vetoed this bill on the grounds that it gave deliberate sanction to the practice of tacking upon appropriation bills legislation not relevant to the expenditure appropriated. Congress tried again in June, with a similar bill, only to meet with another veto. Hayes was as successful with these vetoes as with those in the previous session.

Since 1880 was a presidential election year, the question of Hayes's successor became important. His repeated denial of a desire for a second term was finally taken seriously; according to the *Philadelphia Press* he told a prominent Republican that he could not even consider himself a dark horse candidate. At the Chicago convention in June, a struggle set in. The most likely nominee appeared to be General Grant, for whom a movement for a third term had developed, but John Sherman, Hayes's favorite, the perennial James G. Blaine, Senator George F. Edmunds of Vermont, William Windham of Minnesota, and Elihu Washburne, Grant's former mentor from Illinois, contested the general's claims. Championed by party bosses like John A. Logan and especially Conkling, Grant was long in the lead. "When asked what state he hails from, our sole reply shall be, he comes from Appomattox and its famous apple tree," said Conkling, who nominated him. But his nomination depended on the adoption of the unit rule, which Conkling was unable to force the convention to accept, and in the end Grant's opponents, determined to prevent his success, united on James A. Garfield as a dark horse candidate. In order to give recognition to both factions of the party, since Garfield was a Half-Breed, as the followers of Blaine were called, Chester A. Arthur, the representative of the Stalwarts, the partisans of Conkling, and more active radicals, was chosen for vice president.

The nominations were good ones. Garfield had long been a power in the Republican party. A foe of slavery, the Ohioan had really been born in a log cabin and, as a onetime barge driver, could benefit from a campaign biography entitled *From Canal Boy to President*. Scholar, general, congressman, he had served on the electoral commission, and though his relations with Hayes had often been strained, the two were not very different. Justus Doeneke, the chronicler of his presidency, describes him as "both tall and handsome, possessing a full beard, bright grey eyes, and dark brown hair with patches of red." Although the choice of Chester Arthur for second place was often ascribed to Conkling, he actually had nothing to do with it; the Stalwart was selected to balance the ticket. Although Hayes had dismissed Arthur as collector, according to his biographer George Frederick Howe, "he was a dominating figure in any group," a practical politician who had had a distinguished career in New York as wartime quartermaster general, inspector general, and engineer in chief, and he became a capable president.

Even though Sherman lost, Hayes was satisfied. The convention had endorsed his administration, and Conkling had been defeated. Garfield's nomination was the best that was possible, he thought, and he was pleased with the platform's praise of his accomplishments and the "purity and patriotism" of his career. Viewing Arthur's candidacy with equanimity, he considered it merely a sop thrown to Conkling emphasizing the completeness of his defeat. It was also pleasing to hear from William Henry Smith, who was in Chicago, that some of the delegates had voiced the opinion that it would have been wise for the convention, despite his refusal, to have chosen the incumbent again. The failure of the Democrats to renominate Tilden and endorsing General Winfield S. Hancock instead was another source of satisfaction.

Garfield came to Washington immediately after the convention. Spending two hours with the president and taking dinner with him, he engaged in a long conversation. The two had long enjoyed friendly relations, and despite occasional rifts, appreciated each other. Hayes told Garfield he was sure to win, and promised to do what he could to help the candidate, whom he considered ideally fitted for the presidency because of his rise from a humble origin. Privately, however, he admitted that the final issue was in doubt.

The much-traveled president was again often absent from Washington. Late in March he went to New York to the opening of the Metropolitan Museum of Art, dined at John Jacob Astor's mansion, and had photographs taken. Then he went to Philadelphia to deliver a speech at a memorial for General George G. Meade. In June he attended the commencement exercises at Kenyon College and in July received an honorary doctorate at Yale. Stopping in New York on the way back, he was entertained by Gustav Schwab, the representative of the North German Lloyd Steamship Company, and had dinner aboard the steamship *Mosel.* As a proud veteran, he especially enjoyed military reunions, like the great gathering of former soldiers at Columbus on August 11 and at the meeting of the Twenty-third Regiment at Canton in September, at both of which he delivered popular talks. Then he planned the biggest trip of all, a journey to the Pacific Coast. Accompanied by Lucy, Ruddy, General Sherman, and Secretary Ramsey, he traveled from the end of August to the beginning of November, the first president to visit the Pacific states. At frequent stops, in San Francisco, Portland, Seattle, Sacramento, and elsewhere, he delivered speeches extensively reported in the newspapers, and was gratified by the enthusiastic reception he received. His popularity was evident as governors and mayors welcomed him; he went sightseeing, and enjoyed his stay in the West so much that he decided to remain ten days longer than planned.

When he came back, the election was over, and, much to his satisfaction, the Republicans had won. Unlike four years earlier, they had secured both a popular and electoral college majority, a result that might well be considered an endorsement of the Hayes administration. The president had saved the Republican party from destruction, planted it on the solid rock of good government, and made possible Garfield's election, asserted the *Chicago Tribune*, and many observers agreed.

As during the first two years, Hayes had considerable trouble with his Indian policy. In September 1879 a Ute uprising had to be put down. The Indians killed N. C. Meeker, the agent at White River and took his wife and daughters prisoners. Fortunately for Hayes, Secretary Schurz managed to negotiate with the Utes, especially with Chief Ouray, and succeeded in preventing the enraged citizens of Colorado from taking revenge. When the whites began to invade the Indian Territory, present-day Oklahoma, the president issued several proclamations to stop them. Finally he ran into trouble with the Poncas. An inoffensive tribe whose territory in Nebraska had by mistake been given to the Sioux, they were resettled in the Indian Territory in a trip that amounted to another Trail of Tears. When the area given to them proved unsatisfactory, they were moved to a better one; several Poncas, however, attempted to return to their original home. Led by Chief Standing Bear, who was carrying the remains of his grandson with him, they were arrested by the army but aided by reformers, obtained a writ of habeas corpus in Omaha, and were freed. Secretary Schurz, however, contending that the Supreme Court would not entertain the suit, still refused to let them return, and he now became the chief target of the opposition, although he had called attention to the Poncas' wrongs in the first place. Hayes, who thought Schurz had been most shamefully treated, nevertheless realized that a great injustice had been done to the tribe. He appointed a commission, which recommended a compromise involving compensation to the Poncas, with those who wished to return being allowed to do so, and permitting those who wanted to stay to remain in the Indian Territory. In the president's report to Congress on the matter, in which he accepted the commission's findings, he urged that legislation be passed to give the Poncas lands in severalty and to compensate them for any losses they might have sustained. He also advocated education for young Indians and eventual citizenship. Concluding with a personal apology, he said, "As the chief executive at the time when the wrong was consummated, I am deeply sensible that enough of the responsibility for that wrong justly attaches to me to make it my particular duty and earnest desire to do all I can to give to these injured people that measure of redress which is required alike by justice and by humanity." The message was effective; correspondents assured the president that it would pass into history as a great state paper, and the incident was settled.

The administration's foreign policy was less troublesome. Its chief concern was with the question of an inter-oceanic canal, a problem that became acute when Fernand de Lesseps, the builder of the Suez Canal, organized a company to connect the Caribbean with the Pacific. Hayes, totally opposed to any foreign venture in the Americas, was unwilling to tolerate this violation of the Monroe Doctrine, and in January 1880 ordered the Secretary of the Navy to send two warships to the isthmus to establish naval stations at the Chiriqui Grant in Central America. When he discussed the matter with the cabinet on February 10, it was agreed that any future canal ought to be under American control, a policy the president strongly asserted in a special message to the Senate on March 8. De Lesseps went ahead with his project, however, and tried to win American support by selling securities in the United States and placing American citizens on the company's board. He even offered its chairmanship to Secretary of the Navy Richard W. Thompson, who, much to Hayes's dismay, agreed to serve. The president promptly indicated that Thompson's resignation from the cabinet would be accepted.

In Samoa, the United States refused the island's request for annexation but signed with it a treaty of peace and friendship that contained clauses giving America the right to establish a naval station. In view of the fact that Great Britain and Germany were also interested in the islands, a loose tripartite protectorate was set up.

The Chinese immigration question still had to be solved. After Hayes's veto of the Chinese Immigration Bill, he appointed a commission to negotiate a new treaty with the empire. Headed by James B. Angell, the president of Michigan University, in November 1880 the commission produced a treaty allowing the United States to limit immigration. According to Kenneth E. Davison, the able chronicler of the presidency, it "capped Hayes's successful four-year Asian policy."

On December 6 Hayes delivered his last annual message. After praising the returning prosperity of the country and the advantages of Republican transfers of power as shown in the last election, while regretting the denial of constitutional rights to the blacks, he again stressed his desire for sectional reconciliation. He pleaded for federal funds for education, particularly in the Southern states, and then turned to his favorite subject of civil service reform. Citing the success of competitive examinations in several departments and in post offices and custom houses, he recommended the appropriation of twenty-five thousand dollars for a commission to establish common rules for these tests. Then he inveighed once again against polygamy and proposed that voting and officeholding rights be withheld from all polygamists. He took pride in the successful pursuit of foreign affairs and the efforts to extend the country's international trade, asked for an enlargement of the navy, and suggested the establishment of new courts to deal with the overcrowding of the existing tribunals. As usual, he portrayed the financial condition of the country in a favorable light and recommended the repeal of the Silver Purchase Act. In addition, he called for allotment of lands in severalty for the Indians, new buildings and quarters for the army medical museum and the Department of the Interior, river and harbor improvements, and attention to the needs of the District of Columbia. The message went over well, as did his subsequent speech on December 22 at the Brooklyn New England Society Dinner.

Thus Hayes began his last few months in office during the new year. Starting out on New Year's Day with a letter to Bryan, he asserted, "Nobody ever left the Presidency with less regret, less disappointment, fewer heartburns, or more general content with the result of his term." A splendid New Year's reception, drawing a large crowd in spite of the extremely cold weather (−10°), followed. Lucy, wearing a dress of creamy white silk, trimmed with satin and pearl passementerie, impressed the diplomats, army and navy officers in full uniform, and others present. The Hayeses also tended to dine out, meeting interesting people, such as the historian George Bancroft, who told them of his experiences with the great statesmen of the past.

One of the president's first tasks in the new year was the appointment of a new secretary of the navy in place of Thompson, whose acceptance of the chairmanship of de Lesseps's company had rendered him unacceptable. The new appointee, Nathan Goff, a West Virginia Unionist veteran and lawyer, came with the understanding that Garfield would reappoint him to his position of U. S. district attorney at the end of his term.

The arrangement about the new secretary of the navy was not the only one made with Garfield. Hayes attempted to collaborate with his successor as much as possible, and Garfield responded favorably. The two men exchanged ideas on appointments and sought to be of assistance to each other. The transfer of power was obviously going to be smooth.

A good example of this collaboration was Hayes's previously mentioned unsuccessful attempt to appoint his friend Stanley Matthews to the Supreme Court seat vacated by Justice Noah

Swayne's retirement. When much to his dismay the Senate adjourned before it could confirm the appointee, the president prevailed upon Garfield to renew the appointment. In spite of the strong opposition to Matthews, who as a longtime railroad attorney was suspected of undue partisanship for the rail lines, Garfield complied, and the jurist was confirmed by one vote after a long struggle.

On one subject, however, there was bound to be a difference of opinion. Although the ban on liquor in the White House was popular with various religious figures, Hayes knew that the new president would hardly maintain it. However, believing it had been a wise policy, not only because he approved of it, but also because it would strengthen the Republicans by preempting the appeal of the Prohibition Party, he left a memorandum for Garfield urging the continuance of his practice. Garfield, though badgered by prohibitionists, on Blaine's advice did not comply with the request, as his biographer, Allan Peskin, has shown.

The last presidential receptions seemed to outshine all previous ones in elegance. In January, the New Year's festivity was followed by a dinner for the justices of the Supreme Court on the thirteenth, when Lucy's new porcelain was displayed, and a final one to the diplomatic corps on January 24, when officials of all sorts, members of the Supreme Court, of the cabinet, of Congress, were invited to meet the foreign envoys. Even though no liquor was available at their receptions, the Hayeses were excellent hosts.

The president of course continued on his travels. On February 12, he went to Baltimore to visit Johns Hopkins University and address the banquet of the Baltimore Press Association, and ten days later he came to New York for the presentation of the Egyptian obelisk at the Metropolitan Museum of Art. At all these appearances, he was cordially welcomed and duly honored.

A few governmental matters remained to be taken care of. On February 28, the president transmitted to Congress Dorman B. Eaton's report of the Civil Service Commission concerning competitive examinations. Asserting that the report presented a gratifying statement of the results, Hayes avowed that the subject was one of great importance and recommended the acceptance of the recommendations to authorize these tests. A less agreeable task was his final veto, this time of the Refunding Bill, which was widely considered an attack on the national banking system. The veto was upheld. As for the effort to reverse the verdict on Fitz-John Porter, who had been dismissed upon Pope's charges of misconduct and disobedience after the second Battle of Bull Run, despite pleadings from respected attorneys he left the matter for his successor.

In an interview published in the *New York Times* on March 2, Hayes specified what he thought were the accomplishments of his administration. First of all, he was proud of the pacification of the South; second, he took credit for civil service reform; and third, he congratulated himself for his conservative financial policies. He also believed he had handled the strikes of 1877 well and pointed out the lack of corruption during his term of office.

His assessment was not merely self-praise. Even though hostile newspapers were still carping—"Let him go, guilty conspirator," wrote the *New York Sun*—even Democrats recognized the achievements of the man they had originally derided as a fraud. "I am a Democrat," a West Virginian wrote to him, "doubted your election— have watched your conduct and scanned your course from your inaugural to your 'Ponca' Message, and I am sure you have given us a clean administration, and your fidelity and fair dealing with the lowly and the savage so clearly shown . . . has lifted up our country far above the plane upon which your predecessor had placed it." If this was the endorsement of Democrats, Republicans were naturally proud of the candidate they had elected after such difficulties. George William Curtis was sure that the administration would be counted historically among those of which Americans can be proudest; the Republican Central Committee of the City and County of New York tendered its "thanks to President Rutherford B. Hayes for the Able, Pure, and Brilliant administration which has been endorsed by the people in the election of Genl. James A.

Garfield and Genl. Chester A. Arthur to the position of President and Vice President of the United States," and similar endorsements came from all over the country. The president had indeed come a long way from the dubious beginning of the administration.

In the meantime, Hayes had made arrangements with Garfield for the inauguration. He invited the president-elect to stay with him, but Garfield had already made reservations at Riggs House and suggested that his mother and children board with Hayes, whose dinner invitation he accepted. Hayes in turn agreed to attend Garfield's evening reception on March 4.

On his last evening in the White House, March 3, Hayes gave one last dinner to some fifty people, the president-elect and family, members of the cabinet, the Supreme Court, and sundry officials and friends. On the next day, he went to Garfield's room at Riggs House, drove with him to the White House, and then proceeded with a committee to the Capitol for the inauguration. He attended Garfield's evening reception, and then, after a night's stay in Sherman's house, left for home.

What did Hayes contribute to the presidency? His biographers have generally credited him with unifying the country, though faulting him for not succeeding in safeguarding blacks' rights. This verdict is substantially correct. He was one of the best-educated men to occupy the White House, was honest, evenhanded, and humane. Taking over the scandal-besmirched presidency from General Grant, he reestablished the good reputation of the country's first office and was rewarded with the Republican success of 1880. This was his real achievement.

It may be appropriate to reprint the assessment of the *New York Times* of March 2, 1881:

The record of President HAYES' Administration may be regarded as made up. . . . While it is claimed for the President that his Administration stands in no need of vindication or explanation on its own account, we have obtained from a source that reflects his own feelings and judgment in regard to his official course a statement that may be considered as placing it in the light in which he hopes that it will be viewed by the people of the country hereafter. It will probably be long before the general judgment will be as favorable as that claimed, but the Administration is safe for an honorable place in the memory of the Nation. The last four years have been the period of a somewhat remarkable transition in our affairs. While sectional division and antipathy have by no means wholly disappeared, their harshest features have been softened, and it is easy to mark a decided degree of progress toward renewed nationality. The finances of the country have been restored to the basis of specie with a prospect of permanency, and the national credit has acquired a degree of strength which it never before possessed. The civil service has been in a considerable measure purified and freed from old abuses, and the beginnings of a reform have been made which has sufficient root to acquire a healthy growth if it is favored with fostering care. It is claimed for the President that the progress which has been made in these directions is largely due to his convictions, steadiness of purpose, and firmness in action.

So far as the Southern policy is concerned, the explanation made in behalf of the Administration goes far to qualify its claims to peculiar merit. There is a plea, though it is not put in that form, that the withdrawal of military interposition for the support of State Governments in the South was inevitable. It could no longer effect its purpose, and its maintenance would not be sustained by public sentiment even in the North. This is undoubtedly true, and when President HAYES came into office an embarrassing situation of affairs existed, from which some means of distraction had to be devised.

Whether that adopted by him was the wisest and best may still be questioned, but the task, however it was to be performed, was forced upon him. Its accomplishment was accompanied by professed purposes of conciliation which were to win Southern support for the Government and do much toward mitigating the evils anticipated from leaving the States to themselves. . . .

One of the chief claims made for the Administration to the gratitude of the Nation rests on its civil service policy. For what has been gained we should be truly grateful, and can only hope that it may constitute the foundations of reform of such breath and firmness that they cannot be abandoned.

Although there were also a few criticisms interlaced with this praise, by and large the *Times* did justice to the administration.

# 7

# Retirement

Few presidents enjoyed their retirement years more than Hayes. For some ten years after he left office, he lived an active life, took part in various educational funds, and continued his efforts to effect civil service reform. Above all, he was happy at his retreat in Spiegel Grove, enjoying his family and continuing to live contentedly with his wife.

The trip home from Washington, on which he was escorted by the first Cleveland Troop (Troop A, 107th Cavalry, Ohio National Guard), was marred by a railroad accident at Severn near Baltimore, in which two persons were killed and several wounded. The ex-president and his family, who immediately helped the wounded, escaped unhurt, but the delay caused them to stay over at Altoona. Arriving in Cleveland, they boarded with their niece and nephew and then went on to Clyde, where the welcoming committee met them and escorted them to nearby Fremont. There, a procession led by a band and a large crowd of well-wishers greeted them. The mayor and various officials were present, and Homer Everett delivered a welcoming speech. It was a pleasant homecoming—"a release from bondage," Hayes called it.

Not having practiced his legal profession since his entry into the army, he now engaged in real estate and was chosen director of the First National Bank of Fremont. In addition, he held various trusteeships, one at Western Reserve University, another at the Green Springs Academy, and one at the board of the Oakwood Cemetery. Eventually, he also served on the Slater Fund and the Peabody Foundation, both devoted to education, the Slater Fund particularly to education for freedmen in the South.

His family was doing well. Birch was practicing his profession in Toledo, as a junior partner of two of Justice Noah H. Swayne's sons. Webb, who was still helping at Spiegel Grove, was about to join the Whitney Manufacturing Company in Cleveland. Ruddy was at the Polytechnic Institute in Boston, Fanny had remained in Washington to finish her school year, and Scott was at home. Lucy was active with the animals at the farm, especially the chickens, and the Hayeses soon acquired several pet dogs—a terrier, a Newfoundland, and a shepherd, among others.

To make the family more comfortable, Hayes constantly improved and enlarged his estate at Spiegel Grove. A new brick cistern and a tank with clear water in the attic were finished. So was the parlor, except for a mantel, which was to be made of butternut to correspond to the rest of the wood in the place. He put in a fireplace and installed glass windows at the front door. He also completed the library, after placing some five thousand books on the shelves, and took steps to install gas. By December, there was even a telephone, a still-new invention, which allowed the family to talk to Birch in Toledo.

Although he was definitely out of active politics, Hayes certainly never lost contact with the party. When initiated as a member of the Eugene Rawson Post of the Grand Army of the Republic, he was asked to compare Garfield's problems with his own. He answered that there had been four things he had to do: first, restore constitutional governments to the South; second, bring back prosperity by a return of sound currency; third, reform the civil service; and fourth, strengthen the Republican party. The last point Hayes considered essential for the accomplishment of the others. Always a good Republican, he frequently corresponded with Garfield. Comforted when the new president had controversies with Conkling similar to his own, he welcomed the New Yorker's "suicide," as he called it, when Conkling and his colleague Thomas C. Platt resigned from the Senate. Although he was most critical when Garfield dismissed Merritt, he approved of most of his successor's policies, but was somewhat dismayed by the uncovering of the so-called Star Route Scandal. Located in sparsely settled western areas, star routes were locations in which special contracts assured the delivery of the mail, and in issuing these, individual postal officers had been guilty of fraud. When Hayes's detractors tried to besmear his administration with the scandal, which had begun during his administration, he vigorously defended himself. Pointing out the excellent reputation of his postmaster general, David M. Key, and his second in command, James N. Tyner, he stressed the fact that he had never even known the chief culprit, Thomas J. Brady. As the congressional investigation went on, it became obvious that Hayes was clearly not implicated.

In view of his good relations with Garfield, it is not surprising that he was totally overcome with grief when on July 2 the president was shot in Washington. "The dreadful tragedy at Washington has occupied our thoughts since yesterday morning," he wrote in his diary. "The death of the President at this time would be a national calamity whose consequence we can not now confidently conjecture. Arthur for President! Conkling the power behind the throne!" He feared that the party would be divided and defeated, and the administration would have no moral support whatever. If the president recovered, Hayes thought he would have the stature of Washington and Lincoln, Stalwartism would be ruined, and the great tragedy would turn out to have been good for the country.

As Garfield lingered on, Hayes became more and more worried. "We are in the most distressing anxiety about the President," he wrote. "Mrs. Hayes finds her emotions too strong to control. She breaks down many hours during the anxious days." For a while, Garfield seemed to be getting better, and Hayes wrote an encouraging letter to the family, but the recovery did not last. By the end of August, it was obvious that the president was dying. He passed away on September 19, and Chester A. Arthur became president. Assuring the political reformer, Wayne McVeagh, that he would be happy to visit Garfield's widow and mother, Hayes called the deceased "the best loved man in the United States." Naturally he attended the funeral ceremonies in Washington and Cincinnati. But as time went on, he managed to find some good in the new president, whom he had dismissed in 1878. Firmly denying the charge that he had let Arthur go because of dishonesty, he found the president's first annual message not all bad. "He leans to the right side" on the important questions, civil service, Mormon affairs, and education in the South, Hayes commented, although he did not feel the president went far enough. All in all, however, he believed that when Garfield died the Republican party was left with an unclouded future, and, he mused in May 1882, "It is now said with some asperity, 'This is not a Hayes administration.'"

During the subsequent years of his retirement, Hayes tended to continue his activities in various organizations he headed or to which he belonged, travel widely, and devote himself to his favorite causes. These consisted of a great interest in education, especially industrial education, solving the problems of inequality of wealth, civil service reform, the uplifting of the blacks, and prison reform. He also continued to improve his home at Spiegel Grove and liked to entertain old friends there.

As time went on, he belonged to more and more organizations. Those he enjoyed most were the military associations, the reunions of which he faithfully attended year after year. First and foremost was the Regimental Association of the Twenty-third Ohio Volunteer Infantry, of which he was president, as he was of the Society of the Army of West Virginia. He was also commander in chief of the Military Order of the Loyal Legion of the United States, and joined the Grand Army of the Republic. Educational institutions also kept him busy; he was a member of the board of trustees of the Ohio State University, of Ohio Wesleyan University, of Western Reserve University, and the Peabody Education Fund. Another fund that interested him from its founding was the Slater Education Fund for Freedmen, over which he presided, as well as the National Prison Association and the Garfield Monument Association. The Slater Fund enabled him to attempt actively to further blacks' education in the South and elsewhere, and among his beneficiaries was the young black activist W. E. B. DuBois, whom he found "sensible, sufficiently religious, able, and a fair speaker." For most of these associations, he also delivered speeches at suitable occasions, and he attended many a commencement of colleges with which he was connected.

Much of his time was taken up with travel. "It seems to me you are doing a great deal of visiting," his daughter wrote to him. "Every letter I get says you have just returned from Cincinnati or some other place." Because of his involvement in the Peabody and later the Slater Fund, both located in New York, he often went to the metropolis, where he habitually stayed in the same rooms, numbers 41 and 42, at the Fifth Avenue Hotel. His visits to the city gave him an opportunity to visit his many friends and relatives there, including Carl Schurz, Melvil Dewey, Hamilton Fish, and his cousin Charles L. Mead. Enjoying the picturesque landscape, he also took trips up the Hudson. From New York, it was convenient to journey to New England to see his ancestral towns and renew acquaintances with his remaining relatives. When in his home state, he frequently traveled to Cleveland and Cincinnati, for monthly meetings of the Loyal League in the latter city, and for speeches and visits to his son Webb in the former. In Toledo, he was delighted to see Birch, his daughter-in-law Mary, and his grandson, and in Columbus, he not only spoke frequently but liked to stay with his nephew and niece. In Chicago, he enjoyed seeing his close friend William H. Smith, as well as others in Detroit and Boston. Usually the main orator at various localities on Decoration Day, on July 4, 1883, he spoke impressively in Woodstock, Connecticut. The Slater Fund brought him to Tennessee and the Prison Reform Association to Richmond, Atlanta, and Toronto, where in a widely reported talk he deplored the lack of interest in the cause. It was natural that as ex-president he was everywhere received with great honors and often people turned out to cheer him.

His interest in education went far beyond his membership on the boards of trustees of various universities and schools. Again and again he emphasized his conviction that in addition to the humanities, colleges and schools ought to teach industrial subjects, so that their pupils might be prepared for manual labor. As he wrote in July 1882, "I have for some years been satisfied that the next important step to be taken in progressive improvement of our educational systems is the introduction of instruction in 'the arts by which civilized men live.'" In December 1883, he counseled Whitelaw Reid of the *New York Tribune* to help Blaine with his plan to tax whiskey by confining its income to distribution to the states for universal education. He asserted that he did not oppose the study of the classics, but he advised, "Teach a boy what he will practice when he becomes a man." Believing that a few hours devoted to skilled manual labor to fit the young to make a living with their hands would make them better scholars, he contended that skilled labor as a part of education would build up health, strengthen the mind, and build up character. Maintaining these principles throughout his life, in April 1892 he still delivered an incisive speech on the subject at Wooster, Ohio, and in August one on higher education at Chautauqua.

He was especially interested in education for blacks, largely in the South, but also in Ohio. His activities in the Peabody and Slater Funds partially took care of this concern for the former Confederacy, and he stressed it at the meeting at Lake Mohonk, New York, in 1890. Concerning his home state, he regretted that "for two generations Ohio shared in the oppressive treatment of the African race which prevailed almost everywhere in the United States," and he thought it only right that by legislation for education something should now be done "to uplift the descendants of those who were thus oppressed."

Hayes's concern for uplifting the blacks was closely connected with his hopes for a better racial climate in the South, which he thought he had been able to achieve. "In 1877 I believed that a radical change of policy in regard to the South would bring ultimate safety and prosperity to the colored people and restore good feeling between the hostile sections," he wrote to a well-wisher in February 1883. "The change could be most successfully made by one who represented the victors in the Civil War. Many were disappointed because in the South there were those who did not accept the olive branch. I am *not* of the number." He thought the change did its work, "not instantly, but surely." As evidence mounted that his hopes were not being fulfilled, he nevertheless clung to the idea that education would eventually change this situation.

His interests in the civil rights of blacks were real. Congratulating Justice Harlan for his dissent in the 1883 Civil Rights Cases, in which the majority of the justices had struck down the Civil Rights Act of 1875 guaranteeing equal treatment for blacks in places of public accommodation, he praised Harlan for his "noble" opinion, and in 1890, took part in the calling of a conference at Lake Mohonk largely devoted to African-American affairs. Doubting the old canard that the blacks had no history, he stressed the intelligence of those he had met, remembering that in Bermuda an African American had steered his ship through the most treacherous passage into the harbor, a feat requiring great skill. He rejoined the Mohonk conference for a second year and took note of the blacks at Fisk University constructing telescopes and students at Clark University making carriages and wagons. His activities in the Peabody and Slater Fund were additional examples of his devotion to the cause, and whatever may be said of Hayes's withdrawal of the troops from the Southern statehouses, he certainly was not indifferent to the improvement of the condition of the blacks.

Another one of his causes was the control of the growing inequality of wealth. At a time when theories of laissez-faire predominated, and when it was believed that the iron law of wages could not be disturbed, to say nothing of the ever-present ideas of the survival of the fittest, his concern about this subject was quite unusual and forward-looking. More equal distribution of property was a question he discussed with friends. Believing that in America the development of a permanent aristocracy of inherited wealth should not be allowed, he thought the answer might be a limitation on inheritance with the public the beneficiary of the remainder of the estate. When in May 1886 the riot on Haymarket Square in Chicago brought about a popular revulsion against violence, he was as wholly in favor of suppressing it by force as the general public. "Strikes and boycotts," he had thought for some time, "are akin to war, and can be justified only on grounds analogous to those which justify war, viz., intolerable injustice and oppression." But he still believed that labor did not get its fair share of the wealth it created, and he endorsed President Grover Cleveland's message calling for the establishment of a Commission of Labor to consider and settle industrial disputes. At the funeral in Cleveland of General Arthur F. Devereux, an old acquaintance, he met the railroad magnate Cornelius Vanderbilt, and he could not overlook the inconsistency of permitting such vast power to be vested in the hands of one man. He thought that great wealth must be controlled and railroad kings curbed. He also felt that the taxation system was unfair, taking a much smaller share of the estate of millionaires than of ordinary citizens. "The real difficulty is with the vast wealth and power in the hands of the few and the unscrupulous who represent or control capital," he wrote. "Hundreds of laws of Congress and the state legislatures are in the interests of these men and against the interests of the workingmen." As he summed it up, "Lincoln was for a government of the people. The new tendency is 'a government of the rich, by the rich, and for the rich.'" This type of social conscience was rare and marked Hayes as an early progressive.

His interest in civil service reform never waned. Considering this improvement one of his main achievements as president, he continued to espouse the cause whenever possible. In the first year of his retirement, in September 1881, he wrote to R. U. Johnson, about to publicize the cause in *Scribner's Magazine*, on what he considered to be the most important points of the reform: divorce of the appointing power from the control and influence of members of Congress, competitive examination and tenure during good behavior for all minor appointments, and the prohibition of partisan assessments for officeholders. Looking upon civil service reform as one of the main problems of the time, he criticized Arthur's 1881 message as leaning to the wrong side on the question, but was delighted with the passage of the Pendleton Civil Service Act in 1883, which he considered "a great victory." He thought that he himself had taken the first step in destroying the spoils system by appointing a cabinet not desired by Congress and defeating Conkling, especially as the ending of the New Yorker's political life followed. Paying his costly dues of five hundred dollars to the Civil Service League in 1885, he believed the spoils system was held somewhat in check by "an honest reform President," as he referred to Grover Cleveland. Whenever musing about the achievements of his administration, he numbered the reform among them.

Prison reform was a cause he had already espoused when governor. During his retirement, as president of the National Prison Association, which was reorganized in September 1883, he attended its annual meetings in various cities, delivered speeches, and furthered the cause. At the congress in Atlanta in 1886, he debated the convict lease system, and the following year spoke extensively at the meeting in Toronto, where, at church on Sunday, he enjoyed a prison reform sermon. In November 1888, he addressed a large group in Chicago on the topic of prison reform, and in 1891 opened the prison congress in Pittsburgh. Furthering the cause whenever he could, he never lost interest in the improvement of prison conditions.

Hayes, though not a member of any church, had always gone to Sunday services, especially as his wife was a convinced Methodist. He was the vice president of the Bible Society of his county, believing as he did that Christianity was the best faith in the world and that it was a great mistake not to support the religion of the Bible. He contributed to the construction of a Methodist church in Fremont, and when it burned down in 1888, he was active in raising funds for its rebuilding.

His interest in temperance caused him to continue popularizing his views. Believing that prohibition was a mistake, he felt that the cause could only be promoted by education, example, persuasion, and religion. Thus he took no part for or against any prohibition amendments to the Constitution and wrote, "Unity and harmony among the friends of temperance are, in my judgment, of more importance than particular measures." But his devotion to abstinence never flagged.

Although he repeatedly asserted that he was out of politics for good, he took a deep interest in public affairs. In 1883, he was most anxious for the defeat of the Democratic candidate for governor of Ohio, Judge George Hoadly. The judge had attacked him by charging that he had been made commander of the Loyal League by trickery, to say nothing of Hoadly's service as counsel for Tilden during the disputed election campaign. Hayes even asked Schurz to come and deliver some speeches in Ohio to win back the German Americans, who were disaffected because of the prohibition issue, but the effort was in vain, since Hoadly was elected. In 1884, while favoring the nomination of Sherman, he loyally supported Blaine, even though his friend Schurz, whom he assured of his continuing friendship, deserted the party and came out for Grover Cleveland, the Democratic candidate. When Cleveland won, Hayes was worried that he would turn back the clock in the South and reverse progress in civil service reform. But he had no real prejudice against the new president; in fact, he maintained that he had a good deal of faith in him. Notwithstanding his belief in civil service rules, he asked Schurz to interfere with Cleveland for various appointments, saw the president in person, and came away with his good impressions confirmed.

His dealings with Cleveland did not lessen his support of the Republican party. In 1888 he naturally backed the Republican, Benjamin Harrison, an old acquaintance, although he had again favored the candidacy of Sherman. Congratulating Harrison on his inaugural address, he expressed the opinion that it equaled the best and would rank with Jefferson's and Lincoln's. He also liked the new cabinet. When he met the president in April 1889 at the New York centennial of Washington's inauguration, he found that Harrison was most agreeable and a great speaker. Although in 1890 the Democrats elected James E. Campbell governor of Ohio, Hayes was so pleased with Campbell's inaugural address that he praised him for mentioning topics like home rule for the cities, ballot reform, and money for education, questions in which he was especially interested. He was of course delighted with the election of his friend William McKinley the following year and presided at the new governor's inauguration.

During the entire period of his retirement, Hayes loved to reflect on his career, his achievements as president, and his accomplishments during his wartime service. Again and again, he wrote about it to friends, entered reminiscences in his diary, and commemorated the anniversaries of the battles in which he had taken part. Eagerly collecting favorable mention of his record, he carefully noted down flattering compliments about his achievements. To be told in Atlanta in November 1886 that the South owed him a debt greater than to any man since George Washington and that all agreed he had been the first to take the course that had restored harmony between the sections delighted him, as did the writer and civil service reformer

George W. Curtis's approval of his work for civil service reform. He was equally pleased when he heard that an observer had become convinced that neither Tilden in 1876 nor Cleveland in 1884 were elected because the suppression of the black vote in at least five Southern states deprived the Republicans of their votes. During a visit from McKinley in September 1885, he heard with satisfaction that there was a rapidly increasing appreciation of his administration and a diminishing tendency to abuse him personally. He noted that he was often mentioned as one of the few presidents, perhaps the only one, who left his administration stronger than he had found it. He himself believed that he had left the country united, prosperous, and harmonious, uniting both the party and North and South, and of regaining Congress for the Republicans. These achievements, he was certain, were due to his civil service and financial policies, and he felt the Republican victory in 1880 fully vindicated him. As for the war, which he considered "the divinest war that was ever waged," he reflected upon his exploits at Middletown, Cedar Creek, and elsewhere, loved to read Grant's encomiums of himself in the general's memoirs, and was proud of having been one of the good colonels.

Of course, he also attempted to counter continuing attacks. Charges that he had something to do with the Star Route Scandal were easy to refute. As has been pointed out, he hardly knew the chief suspect, Postmaster Thomas J. Brady, and certainly had no connection with the corruption. Postmaster General Key and his assistant James N. Tyner had assured him of Brady's integrity, and as soon as he found out about the scandal he stopped all practices connected with it. The constantly repeated charges alleging fraud in the counting of the votes in the three Southern states were obviously annoying, but he refuted them by insisting that the observance of the Fifteenth Amendment would have given all three, plus Alabama and Mississippi, to the Republicans. Arguing that if all disputed states had been excluded the Republicans would have had a majority, he cited the election of 1880 as his final justification. Did not the Democrats fail to renominate Tilden, and did not Garfield, one of the visiting statesmen in 1877, carry off the presidential prize? When the death of Justice Bradley raised the question once more in 1892, Hayes, as before, recurred to the disfranchisement of the blacks, as he did a few weeks later when the matter came up again, and he also continued to cite the election of General Garfield as proof of the legitimacy of his administration. He had long since convinced himself of the justice of his cause.

Another activity Hayes continued to enjoy in his retirement was his genealogical research into the Hayes and Birchard families, their relatives, and his wife's ancestry. He corresponded with all who had knowledge of his and Lucy's forebears and traveled often to places where they had lived. In many ways, his genealogical studies paralleled his passion for history, especially local history, which he eagerly pursued, and after its founding in 1884 he joined the American Historical Association.

In spite of his frequent travels, he enjoyed being at his home at Spiegel Grove with his family. Though not all the members of the family were nearby, they were a great source of pleasure for him. Considering his marriage to Lucy the best thing that ever happened to him, he gladly took note of the frequent encomiums of the former first lady. His children continued to do well, Birch and family in Toledo, Webb in Cleveland, Ruddy in the bank in Fremont, and Scott in an electric concern in Cincinnati. Fanny was at home. Lucy was as supportive as ever, but suffered increasingly from rheumatism, and in June 1889 she fell victim to a stroke. Hayes heard the bad news upon his return from a board meeting at Ohio State University in Columbus; he found her sitting in the large low chair at the bay window in the front room on the first floor, paralyzed, and in tears. Soon she could not speak anymore, then became unconscious and died on June 25, with her husband constantly at her bedside holding her hand.

He was disconsolate. His life mate was gone. Acknowledging the many letters of sympathy, including one from the president, he tried to keep busy but could not concentrate on anything but his loss. He tried to continue his routine—the travels, the meetings, the reunions, but of course it was not the same. Month after month he noted the time that had elapsed since his disaster, until, in 1890, he undertook a trip to Bermuda with Fanny, a voyage he enjoyed. Hosted by the governor and local admiral, he appreciated the sights, the island's beauty, and the swimming in the clear waters. Although he still missed Lucy, the trip was a pleasant diversion.

Soon after his return, he attended the Mohonk Conference, and in the summer of 1891 traveled to Kansas, Nebraska, Missouri, and Iowa. That November, the local carbon works burned down, causing a considerable loss for Webb, who had invested in the enterprise. Hayes's travels continued in 1892, including one trip to Washington with Scott, where he visited the old church he had attended with Lucy, spoke several times, and enjoyed the GAR parade. But he was getting old. One after another of his friends were passing away: General Crook, Vice President Wheeler, General Comly, Governor Noyes, Judge T. C. Jones, Chief Justice Waite, Justice Matthews, and others.

Early in 1893, on his way back from Cleveland, Hayes, who had for some time been subject to attacks of vertigo, suffered a heart attack. He managed to reach home, where he was put to bed and died on January 17. According to Charles R. Williams, his last words were, "I know that I am going where Lucy is."

The public funeral services took place on January 21. Following a proclamation to the people of Ohio issued by Governor McKinley, Hayes's last rites were attended by President-elect Cleveland, Governor McKinley, members of the cabinet, and representatives of the various organizations he had headed. Nationwide comments, though not all friendly—the New York Sun could not refrain from mentioning the "theft of the presidency" again—tended to acclaim his accomplishments. The New York Times in a lengthy editorial pointed out that in a difficult and trying time he had acquitted himself with credit, leaving behind him "a record of personal rectitude and of respectable achievement," doing much to "quench the fires of sectional hostility, to allay the animosities of civil strife, and to set the nation upon a new course of peace and prosperity." It was a justified summing up.

# 8

---

# Conclusion

In retrospect, what was the significance of Rutherford B. Hayes? It is obvious that he was one of the most educated of our presidents, an intellectual stimulated by philosophical and other questions, who, as already mentioned, read widely and often. Thorough and comprehensive in his tastes, he perused biographies, histories, and novels, including such classics as Tolstoy's *War and Peace* and Mark Twain's *A Connecticut Yankee in King Arthur's Court*. Shakespeare, Milton, Pope, Byron, Dickens, and many others were steadies, but his favorite was Emerson, whom he had heard speak in person, and whose philosophy appealed to him. Hayes's doctorate of law at Harvard was well merited.

Though not a member of any church and often doubting such religious verities as immortality, Hayes attended services regularly and ended up a good Christian. "I try to be a Christian, or rather I want to be a Christian and help do Christian" work, he wrote in 1890. Free from religious prejudice, he often spoke at Roman Catholic gatherings, was free from the usual anti-Semitism of his time, and believed fervently in the separation of church and state. He saved several culprits, especially women, from the death penalty and bore no personal animosity toward individual Confederates. Optimistic, personable, and easily approachable, he was basically a happy individual.

When this polite and friendly man became president under conditions unequaled until 2000, he was faced with a most difficult situation. Confronted by a party divided into Stalwarts and Half-Breeds, to say nothing of an opposition that disputed his very right to the office, he sought, unlike his twenty-first-century successor, to conciliate the various factions. Failing to carry out Stalwart programs by withdrawing the troops from Southern statehouses and abandoning the Republican governors of South Carolina and Louisiana, he nevertheless refused to abandon their program of aid to the freedmen by insisting on the observance of the Reconstruction amendments. In foreign policy likewise, Hayes did not give in to extremist demands to wage war against Mexico. Although he vetoed the Chinese Exclusion Act, he counseled revision of the existing treaty, again showing his moderation. And even in furthering civil service reform, he was not at all inattentive to occasional special demands for patronage.

In short, aware of the tenuous nature of his election, he knew how to bridge over various disputes and thus heal the serious differences between factions, sections, and parties. As he himself frequently mentioned, the failure of the Democrats to renominate Tilden and the subsequent victory of the Republicans with General Garfield was the final tribute to his policies. His significance, then, lies in his ability to overcome factionalism and exercise power in such a way that the dubious nature of his election could eventually be forgotten.

# Milestones

1822 Born in Delaware, Ohio, son of Rutherford Hayes, Jr., and Sophia Birchard.

1824 In the United States, contested election of John Q. Adams.

1838–1842 Attends Kenyon College.

1840 In the United States, election of William Henry Harrison.

1843–1845 Attends Harvard Law School.

1845–1848 Practices law in Lower Sandusky (Fremont).

1846–1848 In the United States, war with Mexico.

1849–1858 Practices law in Cincinnati.

1850 In the United States, Compromise of 1850.

1852 Marries Lucy Webb.

1852 Campaigns for Whig candidate, Winfred Scott.

1854 In the United States, Kansas-Nebraska Act; birth of Republican party.

1856 Campaigns for Republican candidate, John C. Frémont.

1858–1860 Elected Cincinnati city solicitor.

1860 Defeated for reelection as city solicitor; campaigns for Abraham Lincoln.

1861 In the United States, secession and Civil War.

1861–1865 Serves in the army, rising from major to major general.

1864 Elected to Congress from 2nd District in Cincinnati.

1865 In the United States, Civil War ends; Lincoln assassinated.

1865–1867 Serves in Congress.

1868–1872 Elected governor of Ohio.

1868 In the United States, impeachment of President Andrew Johnson; election of U. S. Grant to the presidency.

1872–1875 Retirement in Fremont.

1875–1877 Third term as governor of Ohio.

1876   Hayes's nomination and disputed election to the presidency.
1877   Electoral Commission awards presidency to Hayes.
1877   Withdraws troops from Southern states.
1878   Struggle with Conkling concerning New York Custom House.
1879   Succeeds against Conkling concerning New York Custom House.
1879   Blocks effort to end federal supervision of elections.
1880   Election of Garfield.
1881   Retirement.
1881   In the United States, assassination of Garfield; Chester A. Arthur becomes president.
1884   Supports James G. Blaine; election of Grover Cleveland.
1888   Supports Benjamin Harrison.
1889   Lucy Webb Hayes's death.
1893   Death of Rutherford B. Hayes in Fremont.

# Selected Bibliography

This book relies heavily on Charles Richard Williams's excellent five-volume edition of the *Diary and Letters of Rutherford B. Hayes*, from which I have quoted and paraphrased. T. Harry Williams's *Hayes: The Diary of a President, 1875–1881* was also helpful. Previous biographies of Hayes, particularly those of Ari Hoogenboom and Harry Barnard, are indispensable, as are the accounts of the presidency by Hoogenboom and Kenneth H. Davison. I have also used the campaign biographies of J. Q. Howard and Russell H. Conwell, as well as T. Harry Williams's account of the war years.

### BOOKS

Abbott, Lyman. *Silhouettes of My Contemporaries.* Garden City, N.Y.: Doubleday, 1927.

*Annual Message of the Governor of Ohio . . . 1868, 1870, 1871, 1872, 1877.* Columbus, Ohio: State Printers, 1868, 1870, 1871, 1872, 1877.

*Appleton's Annual Cyclopedia 1877.* New York: Appleton & Co., 1878.

Barnard, Harry. *Rutherford B. Hayes and His America.* Indianapolis: Bobbs-Merrill, 1954.

Barnes, Thurlow Weed. *Memoir of Thurlow Weed.* Boston: Houghton Mifflin, 1884.

Belmont, Perry. *An American Democrat: The Recollections of Perry Belmont.* New York: Columbia University Press, 1940.

Bonadio, Felice A. *North of Reconstruction: Ohio Politics 1865–1970.* New York: New York University Press, 1970.

Brown, Harry James, and Frederick D. Williams, eds. *The Diary of James A. Garfield.* 4 vols. East Lansing: Michigan State University Press, 1967–1981.

Bruce, Robert Vance. *1877: Year of Violence.* Indianapolis: Bobbs-Merrill, 1959.

Carpenter, William Henry, and T. S. Arthur. *The History of Ohio.* Philadelphia: Claxton, 1872.

Conwell, Russell H. *Life and Public Services of Gov. Rutherford B. Hayes.* Boston: B. B. Russell, 1876.

Cox, Jacob D. *Military Reminiscences of the Civil War.* New York: Scribner's Sons, 1910.

Crook, George. *See* Schmitt, Martin F.

Davis, J. Lucy Webb. *Lucy Webb Hayes: A Memorial Sketch.* Cincinnati: Cranston A. Stone, 1890.

Davison, Kenneth E. *The Presidency of Rutherford B. Hayes.* Westport, Conn.: Greenwood Press, 1972.

Dix, Morgan, ed. *Memoirs of John Adams Dix.* 2 vols. New York: Harper & Bros., 1883.

Fast, Robert Ellsworth. *The History and Government of West Virginia.* Morgantown, W. Va.: Acne, 1901.

Foraker, Joseph Benson. *Notes of a Busy Life.* 3d ed., 2 vols. Cincinnati: Stewart & Kidd Co., 1917.

Garfield, James A. *See* Harry James Brown and Frederick D. Williams.

George, Mary Carl. *Zachariah Chandler: A Political Biography.* East Lansing: University of Michigan Press, 1969.

Gibson, A. M. *A Political Crime.* New York: William Gottsberger, 1885.

Hayes, Rutherford B. *The Papers of Rutherford B. Hayes.* Hayes Memorial Library, Fremont, Ohio. Microfilm. *See also* Louis D. Rubin Jr.; Charles Richard Williams; and T. Harry Williams.

Hearn, Chester. *Six Years of Hell: Harpers Ferry During the Civil War.* Baton Rouge: Louisiana State University Press, 1996.

Hinsdale, Burke A. *History and Civil Government of Ohio.* Chicago: New York Werner School Co., 1896.

Hoogenboom, Ari. *The Presidency of Rutherford B. Hayes.* Lawrence, Kans.: University Press of Kansas, 1988.

———. *Rutherford B. Hayes: Warrior and President.* Lawrence, Kans.: University Press of Kansas, 1995.

Howard, J. Q. *The Life and Public Services of Rutherford B. Hayes.* Cincinnati: Robert Clarke, 1876.

Howells, William Dean. *Sketch of the Life and Character of Rutherford B. Hayes.* New York: Hurd & Houghton, 1876.

Jordan, David M. *Roscoe Conkling of New York: Voice in the Senate.* Ithaca, N.Y.: Cornell University Press, 1971.

Moore, Frank. *The Rebellion Record.* New York: Putnam, 1861–1863; Van Nostrand, 1864.

Nevins, Allan, ed. *Selected Writings of Abram S. Hewitt.* New York: Columbia University Press, 1937.

Polakoff, Ian. *The Politics of Inertia: The Election of 1876 and the End of Reconstruction.* Baton Rouge: Louisiana University Press, 1973.

Poore, Benjamin Perley. *Perley's Reminiscences: 60 Years in the National Metropolis.* 2 vols. Philadelphia: Hubbard Bros., 1886.

Richardson, James D. *Messages and Papers of the Presidents.* 9 vols. New York: Bureau of National Literature and Art, 1908.

Richardson, Leon Burr. *William S. Chandler, Republican.* New York: Dodd, Mead, 1940.

Robinson, Lloyd. *The Stolen Election: Hayes versus Tilden 1876.* Garden City, N.Y.: Doubleday, 1968.

Roseboom, Eugene H., and Francis Phelps Weisenburger. *A History of Ohio.* New York: Prentice-Hall, 1934.

Rubin, Louis D., Jr., ed. *Teach the Freemen: The Correspondence of Rutherford B. Hayes and the Slater Fund for Negro Education 1881–1887.* 2 vols. Baton Rouge: Louisiana State University Press, 1959.

Ryan, Daniel. *A History of Ohio with Biographical Sketches of Her Governors.* Columbus, Ohio: A. H. Smythe, 1888.

Schmitt, Martin F., ed. *General George Crook, the Autobiography.* Norman, Okla.: University of Oklahoma Press, 1960.

Seitz, Don C. *The Dreadful Decade: Detailing Some Phases of the History of the United States from Reconstruction to Resumption.* Indianapolis: Bobbs-Merrill, 1926.

Shannon, Fred A. *The Centennial Years: A Political and Economic History of America from the Late 1870s to the Early 1890s.* Garden City, N.Y.: 1967.

Sherman, John. *John Sherman's Recollections of Forty Years in the House, Senate, and Cabinet.* 2 vols. Chicago: The Warner Co., 1895.

Stackpole, Edward James. *Sheridan in the Shenandoah: Jubal Early's Nemesis.* Harrisburg, Pa.: Stackpole Co., 1961.

Statler, Boyd B. *West Virginia in the Civil War.* Charleston, W. Va.: Education Foundation, 1966.

Taylor, Joe Gray. *Louisiana Reconstructed 1863–1877.* Baton Rouge: Louisiana State University Press, 1974.

United States, 45th Congress, 3d Session, H. R. Misc. Doc. 31. *Presidential Election Investigation. Testimony Taken by the Select Committee on Alleged Frauds in the Presidential Election of 1876.* 5 vols. Washington D.C.: Government Printing Office, 1879.

Williams, Charles Richard. *The Life of Rutherford Birchard Hayes, 19th President of the United States.* Columbus: Ohio State Archaeological and Historical Society, 1914.

———, ed. *Diary and Letters of Rutherford B. Hayes.* 5 vols. Columbus: Ohio Archaeological and Historical Society, 1922.

Williams, T. Harry. *Hayes of the Twenty-third: The Civil War Volunteer Officer.* New York: Alfred A. Knopf, 1965.

———, ed. *Hayes: The Diary of a President.* New York: David McKay, 1964.

Wise, John S. *Recollections of Thirteen Presidents.* Reprint. Freeport, N. Y.: Books for Libraries Press, 1968.

Woodward, C. Vann. *Reunion and Reconstruction: The Compromise of 1877 and the End of Reconstruction.* Garden City, N.Y.: Doubleday, 1956.

## ARTICLES

Bassett, John Spencer. "The Significance of the Administration of Rutherford B. Hayes." *South Atlantic Quarterly* 17 (July 1918): 198–206.

Clendenen, Clarence C. "President Hayes's 'Withdrawal' of the Troops—An Enduring Myth." *South Carolina Historical Magazine* 70 (October 1969): 240–50.

Davison, Kenneth E. "The Nomination of Rutherford B. Hayes for the Presidency." *Ohio History* 77 (1968): 95–110.

De Santis, Vincent P. "President Hayes's Southern Policy." *Journal of Southern History* 21 (November 1955): 477–94.

Garrison, Curtis W., ed. "Slater Fund Beginnings: Letters from General Agent Atticus G. Haywood to Rutherford B. Hayes." *Journal of Southern History* 5 (May 1939): 223–45.

Geer, Emily Apt. "Lucy Webb Hayes and Her Family." *Ohio History* 77 (1968): 33–57.

Marchman, Watt P. "Rutherford B. Hayes, Attorney at Law." *Ohio History* 77 (1968): 6–32.

Nichols, Jeanette Paddock. "Rutherford B. Hayes and John Sherman." *Ohio History* 77 (1968): 125–38.

Parker, Wyman W. "President Hayes's Graduation Speeches." *Ohio State Archaeological and Historical Quarterly* 63 (1951): 135–46.

Pennanen, Gary. "Public Opinion on the Chinese Question, 1876–1879." *Ohio History* 77 (1968): 139–46.

Peskin, Allan. "Garfield and Hayes: Political Leaders of the Gilded Age." *Ohio History* 77 (1968): 111–25.

Porter, Daniel. "Governor Rutherford B. Hayes." *Ohio History* 77 (1968): 58–75.

Sternstein, Jerome L. "The Sickles Memorandum: Another Look at the Hayes-Tilden Election-Night Conspiracy." *Journal of Southern History* 22 (August 1966): 342–57.

Williams, T. Harry, and Stephen E. Ambrose. "The 23rd Ohio." *Civil War Times Illustrated* 3 (March 1965): 23–25.

# Index

# ABOUT THE AUTHOR

Hans L. Trefousse, Distinguished Professor of History Emeritus at Brooklyn College and the Graduate Center of the City University of New York, is a specialist in the history of the Civil War and Reconstruction. He is the recipient of various grants, including a Guggenheim Fellowship. The author of biographies of leading figures of the period as well as works on the Pearl Harbor attack, he is now working on a book on the reputation of Abraham Lincoln during his administration.

**DATE DUE**

| | | | |
|---|---|---|---|
| | | | |
| | | | |
| | | | |
| | | | |
| | | | |
| | | | |
| | | | |
| | | | |
| | | | |
| | | | |
| | | | |
| | | | |
| | | | |
| | | | |
| | | | |
| | | | |

JAN    '08